Letters from the Earth
A Memoir

Nancy Flinchbaugh

Copyright © 2018 by Nancy Flinchbaugh (Higher Ground Books & Media)
All rights reserved. No part of this publication may be reproduced may be reproduced in any form, stored in a retrieval system, or transmitted in any form, or by any means (electronic, mechanical, photocopying, recording or otherwise) without prior permission by the copyright owner and the publisher of this book.

Unless otherwise noted, all Scripture quotations are from the Holy Bible, New King James Version. Copyright © 1979, 1980, 1982, 1995.

Higher Ground Books & Media
Springfield, Ohio.
http://highergroundbooksandmedia.com

Printed in the United States of America 2018

Other Books by Nancy Flinchbaugh

Revelation in the Cave
Revelation at the Labyrinth

Follow Nancy on her websites at:

spiritualseedlings.com
nancyflinchbaugh.com

And on Facebook at:
Nancy Flinchbaugh, Author

Contact her at:
Nancy.Flinchbaugh@gmail.com

Letters from the Earth
A Memoir

Nancy Flinchbaugh

What they're saying about Letters from the Earth

Dancing between humor, excitement, and tragedy, Nancy cleverly educates and subtly challenges her audience to become one with each other and Mother Earth through her letters from Gaia.
> Pastor Adam Banks, First Baptist Church, Springfield, Ohio. 2016 Graduate, Princeton Theological Seminary

Nancy receives these messages from the ears of her heart. She sees Mother Earth with the eyes of her soul. Her writing lends us hope that we too can listen to the symphony of the heavens and see the tapestry of nature, concealed from mortal sight, but visible to the inner eye.
> Farzana Moon, Muslim poet, historian and playwright, author of fourteen books on history and religion

Letters from the Earth is *a a beautiful reflection on the truth that we live in a world that is full of animation. We all are sent messages from our Mother Earth unceasingly through her creatures and landscapes. This book reminds us to become still and listen deeply to receive Her abundant love letters. "*
> Barb Davis, spiritual director and teacher, Spirituality Network of Columbus

Letters from the Earth gently prods us to awaken to all that is praiseworthy on our planet and in our lives, despite the many disturbing ecological and political facts of our time. Ultimately, Letters from the Earth is about exercising hope in the resilience and brilliance of our planet.
> Bre Jeffrey, traveler

A description of the beauty of nature with sunrise and sunset, mountains and greenery and a variety of living beings enjoying and dancing with the resources provided by Mother Earth (Gaia). It matches the Hindu philosophy which views all creation as part of God. The book also explores how we are changing and destroying our environment. We need to preserve the Earth and keep it livable for future generations. I fully support the author's sentiments.
> Dr. Ravi Khanna, Hindu Medical Oncologist, Retired

In Letters from the Earth, Nancy shares wisdom received through deeply contemplative spiritual practice. As she conveys Gaia's voice from a larger view, a dancing force of life emerges through it. An ancient yet present and personal source of love reminds those dedicated to planetary stewardship to celebrate. This book brings you close to the heart of our Earth, ground of our being. Her words open us to passionately appreciating the gift of life in all experience, whether in grief or in delight.
> Karen Jeffers-Tracy, Grandmother, Librarian, Climate Science Educator

<u>Letters from the Earth</u> *is not only wonderful devotional reading; it is also prophetic and makes a compelling contribution to our collective efforts to steward God's creation. What impressed me most is the evidence found in the letters and responses that the author is really listening, growing and becoming exactly the person God has called her to be*
> Rev. Dr. Ken Whitt, American Baptist Pastor and Spiritual Director, author of *Halfway to Heaven*

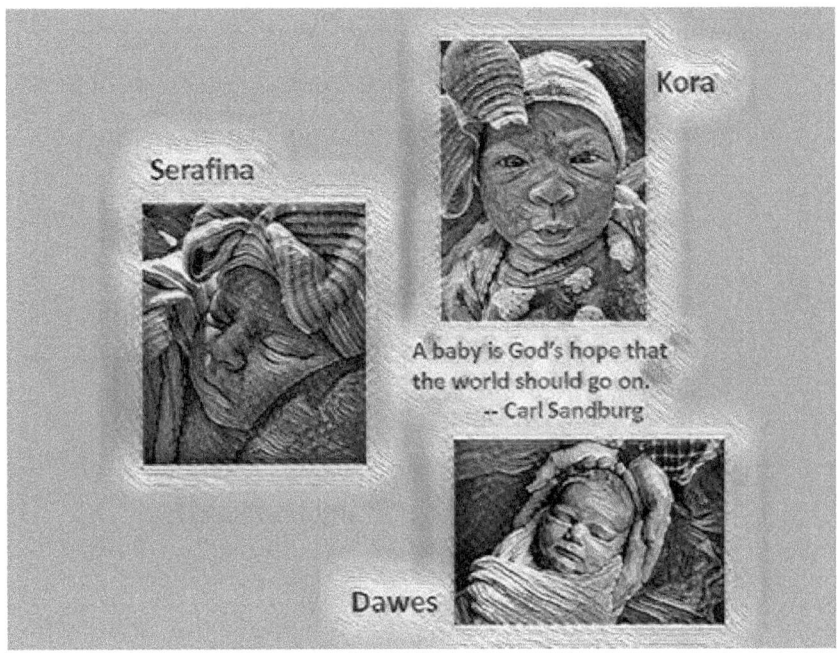

Dedication

To these 2018 newborns and their parents, offering both hope and a call to action:

    Kora Kathleen Copeland born August 2, 2018
        to Candace and Jordan Copeland
    Nathaniel Dawes Tamplin born July 30, 2018
        to Carla and Zach Tamplin
    Serafina Lucia Migliozzi Voltz born August 9, 2018 to Tim and Andrea Migliozzi Voltz

&

To those who inspire me by their diligent work to build political will to address climate change,
I stand with the 100,000+ members and diligent staff of Citizens' Climate Lobby and especially.
Marshall Saunders (founder), Mark Reynolds (executive director), Doug Bell (Ohio State Coordinator), Steve Schlather (Clark County Coordinator and my husband).

TABLE OF CONTENTS

What they're saying about Letters from the Earth........7

Dedication..9

Prelude...13

The Original Letter from the Earth – May, 2015..........19

A Letter from the Earth at Old Man's Cave – July, 2015..27

A Letter from the Earth at Lakeside – August, 2015..33

A Letter from the Earth While Praying with a Holy Icon- Late August, 2015..39

A Letter from the Earth: Garden Party-September 13, 2015..45

A Letter from the Earth Concerning CultureFest- September 30, 2015...53

A Letter from the Earth Concerning Travels in Ireland- October 19, 2015...59

A Letter from the Earth about the Great Coming Together-December 6, 2015.....................................67

A letter from the Earth on Christmas Day 2015.........75

A Letter from the Earth about the Darkness in the Winter-January 11, 2016..81

A Letter from the Earth about the Cold-January 14, 2016..87

A Letter from the Earth at the Beach-January 18, 2016..91

A Letter from the Earth about Love at the Beach- January 19, 2016..95

A Letter from the Earth about Sorrow at the Beach-January 20, 2016...101

A Letter from the Earth about Avoiding Blizzard Travel-January 22, 2016...105

A Letter from the Earth Encouraging Me to Continue Listening-January 25, 2016.....................................109

A Letter from the Earth concerning the Animals-January 26, 2016...113

A Letter from the Earth Concerning a Walk in the Arboretum-January 31, 2016...................................117

A Letter from the Earth Concerning Death-February 2, 2016...121

A Letter from the Earth concerning Natural Healing-February 10, 2016...127

A Letter from the Earth on Valentine's Day-February 14, 2016...131

A Letter from the Earth calling for Connection-February 20, 2016...135

A Letter from the Earth about the Dance-March 5, 2016...139

A Letter from the Earth Concerning Learning with Mary Anna-March 8, 2016..143

A Letter to the Reader from Nancy........................147

Acknowledgements...153

Resources..155

Prelude

As I write this introduction, I'm sitting in my son's home in Seattle. About the same time last year, my husband and I visited here and I received my first letter from the Earth. As I sit at his dining room table, gazing out at the sunshine and the flowering spring of the U District, I consider all that transpired in the past year. I feel gratitude for this beautiful region that led to my first letter and a sense of grounding for the path that brought me to the place of deep listening. I also feel a sense of awe, wonderment and evolving love for my friend, Gaia, who continues to teach me about life.

You see, gradually, over my life, I fell in love with God and her created world. Like a mystery unraveling into my consciousness, this awareness led and grounded me, even as I wandered with many questions and pondering. From an early age, growing up in the Christian church as a preacher's kid, I sought my own spiritual path, questioning God. When I felt God's presence answering, I committed my life to serve God and people. Not sure what this would mean, I asked for God to unfold the meaning of life to me. I majored in sociology and religion in college and felt an evolving call to work for social justice and peace, finding many ways to do that in my work and avocations. But more recently, caring for the Earth became important to me.

In 2011, I began an eighteen-month class on Leading Contemplative Small Groups and Retreats with the Shalem Institute for Formation, a wonderful organization teaching both lay leaders and clergy ways to integrate contemplative practices and spiritual direction into Christian communities. During this class, I started meditating daily. Meditation connects me with the Earth.

I learned a practice in my Shalem class called "Lectio Divina" (divine reading). This practice, originally designed for reading scripture, calls one to listen contemplatively. We were encouraged to listen to the Word of God in nature. So first, you read nature (*lectio*) and look for something that jumps out at you or "shimmers". Then you meditate (*meditatio*) what meaning this has for your life. Afterwards, you pray (*oratio*) about the meaning. And finally, you just sit into silence, and contemplate (*contemplativo*). I really enjoy doing this, and always the earth shares a lesson for my life.

So, I already knew that when I took time to listen, the Earth offered messages to illuminate and guide me on my path. So gradually, I began to realize that whenever I took time to observe and really consider Earth, I could witness miracle after miracle, lesson after lesson, and at the same time, my heart grew heavier as I began to really understand what climate change can mean for life on the planet if we don't do something soon.

Also, my husband and I took an EcoSpirituality class with the Spirituality Network of Columbus, Ohio, where we were encouraged to listen to Earth issues more deeply. We learned about the Anchuar people in Ecuador who are calling the North (Eagle) to awaken to the trauma we are causing to the Earth and to learn from the South (Condor) to become more in sync with the Earth. They envision that the eagle and condor must fly together to heal the Earth.

In this class, artfully led by Spiritual Director Barb Davis, we made Earth Prayer Bracelets. Each bead represented a different aspect of creation, and we were instructed to pray with the bracelet daily. A multi-colored bead represented the people of the Earth, and also our role to care for the Earth. When I first began this prayer practice, I remember fingering the bead and feeling overwhelmed with the challenges of Earth care. I doubted I could do anything significant. But gradually, I discovered there were small steps that I could take. And my path continued to unfold.

We learned about the New Creation Story that helped me consider the incredible miracle that our Earth evolved for 4.7 billion years to reach this point where the Earth has finally "become conscious of itself" through human beings. We viewed a wonderful short film designed for the Anchauar's Awakening the Dreamer movement, called "The Awakening Universe" by Neal Rogin which in 15 minutes, takes us through the incredible creation process and then asks how we could destroy this incredible environment. I later attended their "Awakening the Dreamer" seminar and made a pledge to do what I could.

When I first came out here to the great Northwest to visit my son, he was serving as IT Coordinator for the Lutheran retreat center of Holden Village, high in the Cascade Mountains. I developed a five-day class in contemplative practices with the Earth to present there, as part of a class assignment with Shalem. As I continued to lead contemplative small groups and retreats, I always included the Earth in the practice. As I completed my first novel with a peace theme (*Revelation in the Cave)* and began to consider the next one, I decided on an Earth theme.

In this second novel I write about the earth, I created my main character as a modern-day prophet and heroine who would overcome alcoholic addiction and a life of abuse to speak for the Earth. I named her Thomaseena, after Thomas Berry, the Catholic priest who wrote years ago about the ecological challenge we face. Berry told us that we are now in the Ecozoic Age and that we must change the way we are treating the Earth, or it will be the last age for humans.

When I began a MAMs Book Club Springfield, an offshoot of the group of women in my first novel, I looked for Earth-themed books when it was my turn to select. I felt a deep call to speak for the Earth and to use my voice to join the symphony of similar voices calling out our times. At my Toastmaster's Club, I tried out my voice on this topic, developing speeches and confidence.

I became interested in labyrinths and designed and created a cloth labyrinth with friends that we began to use at our church for walking meditations. We called it the "Living Vine Labyrinth" because the paths were lined with vining leaves and at each turn, there were flowers. I studied under Rev. Lauren Artress, an Episcopal priest and the founder of the modern-day labyrinth movement, becoming a "Certified Labyrinth Facilitator". There I learned that the labyrinth connects us with the Earth.

My husband attended training with the Climate Reality Project, bringing back a wealth of knowledge about the challenges of climate change. He then decided to start a Citizens' Climate Lobby chapter in our town. I joined him and developed great respect for these people creatively calling for bipartisan political will to address climate change. We began writing letters, organizing events, attending conferences and doing whatever we could.

So gradually, I began to realize that my call to serve God and people with my life must include work for the Earth. I began to realize the great jeopardy we will face if we do not address climate change soon. And I have fallen deeper and deeper in love with the Earth as I take the time to listen and explore and serve.

For many years, I journaled daily. Sometimes I dialogue with Jesus and experience God talking to me in this way. So, you can see that when I put pen to paper to receive a letter from the Earth, I listened intently. And when I opened myself to listen, what she said resonated deeply with me. I found her quite nurturing, very surprising and quite encouraging. I felt loved and challenged to continue this path with imagination and wonder.

I began sharing the letters on my website, wanting others to feel the love and encouragement, but not sure how to get the word out there very far. When I first shared my letters from the Earth with my writing coach, Kathie Giorgio, she encouraged me to compose them into a book. So, I began to frame the letters and share the ways they have impacted my life. With great excitement, I realized this would be yet another way for me to care for the Earth. And now, I am ready to share them with you.

My hope is that some of these letters will speak to you. I hope they call you to participate more fully in the dance of life, enjoying the moment and experiencing the incredible miracles of each day. At the same time, I hope they will call you to speak up, to speak out, and to join with other voices calling to preserve the diversity of life that includes us all. For we are a part of a wondrous ecosystem that continues to astound and confound and ground. We are not separate, we are one.

My prayer is that these letters might help you fall in love with our God, the Spirit active in all of creation, and within your very own beating heart.

With great hope and gratitude to my friend, Gaia, who has shared these life giving words to me, I happily now pass them on to you.

Nancy J. Flinchbaugh, April 15, 2016, Seattle, Washington

The Original Letter from the Earth – May, 2015

Introduction

    To put this letter in context, I felt very close to the Earth last year when we visited Seattle in the spring. Shortly after arriving, we drove north to the San Juan Islands where we spent two nights on a small resort. The breathtaking beauty of these waterways and great forests affected my entire being.
    My husband wanted to see the whales, so we went on a whale watching tour. We followed some dolphin pods, observed the sea lions and seals

hanging out on a reef, but hadn't spotted any whales. We learned about these sea creatures and the long migration of the humpback whales from northern waters to the south in their annual journey. We considered the mystery of these sea creatures, whom scientists have discovered have significant intelligence.

On the way back, the boat captain guided the boat on a detour to a location where the whales were recently sighted and turned off the engine. We drifted in the waters between the US and Canada, waiting.

In a little while, we saw a large creature swimming toward our boat. She surfaced and circled us. Our guide told us her name, "Big Mama."

This humpback whale, bigger than a school bus, poked her head out of the water, standing vertically and looked at all of us. "She's curious," our captain told us. Then she disappeared. A few moments later, he said, "She's under our boat." I realized she had the power to turn us upside down. Even the captain seemed a little nervous. "She'll come up over there," he said, pointing to the other side of the boat. We moved to the other side.

And there she surfaced once more, poking just her head up and looked at us. We snapped pictures of her, as she continued to gaze at all of us. For several minutes, she stayed with us, seemingly interested in the earthlings on our boat. After a while, she swam off, and we went back to shore, grateful for this interaction with this huge creature of the sea.

On the way back to Seattle we visited another beach, walking on the sand surrounded with driftwood and the cool Pacific air, blue skies, evergreens and the jagged shoreline. At Deception Pass, we walked across the bridge, high above the beauty and even took a swim in the exhilarating cool waters of Puget Sound. I really enjoyed this time of being in nature and connecting with the Earth.

Once we were back in town, I suggested we do an exercise from Joanna Macy and Chris Johnstone's book, *Active Hope: How to Face the Mess We're in without Going Crazy*. This book talks about our environmental crisis and how to deal with it. For an exercise, she told us to answer the question: "Who am I?" ten times and then to share the answers with each other. We sat around the table at Choco Canyon, an organic bistro, celebrating someone's birthday. I wrote, "I am a woman." "I am part of my family." "I am a child of God." "I am a global citizen…" Through this exercise, I think we all realized our connections with each other and the larger community of humanity and the Earth.

Feeling enthused by the experience, when we returned to my son's house, I suggested that we try another exercise from the book, "Write a letter to yourself from the Earth." We found some paper and set the timer for 15 minutes to write.

As I started to write, I just let my hand go and listened, letting the Earth speak through me. Words gushed out across the page. I laughed. So unexpected, really, and rather delightful, I realized. In a few minutes, the paper filled with a very nice message from the Earth. I remember feeling dazzled.

Afterward, we reassembled to share the results. My son first said, "I didn't do it." I couldn't continue." My husband proceeded to read his rather stern letter, calling us to task for the way we've been harming the Earth. I laughed as I then shared my letter, which was quite a wonderful message of hope to me. I believe Big Mama and my life path led me to this point, to receive.

The Letter

Dear Nancy,

Thank you for noticing me. I love you. We are together -- one -- united. We breathe together. I love you so much.

Thank you for speaking up for me. Don't lose heart. We've been working together a long time. Keep gathering companions. You are not alone. Be positive. Let my Spirit sing through you. Have fun! Dance! So many of my creatures dance. You can, too. There are many more mountains for you to climb and explore.

Speak! Don't be silent. I think you should start a blog. You have many thoughts gushing out of you. Listen. It's coming from beyond you, and we live together. Remember you are an expression of me.

Spend more time with Mary Anna. Seek out earth teachers. You are a teacher. Teach my truth. Don't hold it in anymore. I will open doors and paths for you. Don't be afraid to follow the path of your life into your journey.

Be kind to the people. They're all part of us. Encourage them to get back in touch, but don't push -- just invite. I will wake you up. I will awaken the masses. Let us dance.

See us swaying. Have a new consciousness. Don't consider yourself separate and isolated. Wake up to the beauty of a web containing us all and Dance! I say Dance!

I didn't evolve you into being over 4.7 billion years to have you sit around like lumps on a log. This is a huge experiment and a wonderful dance. Take joy!

I'm sorry if it's not ideal. There is pain and also joy. Take joy. Learn from the pain.

Be real. Keep speaking up. It's not too late.

Love, Gaia

My response

When I first read my letter out loud to my husband and my son, I felt happy and a little astonished.

"It is, isn't it?" I replied.

My son nodded.

I reread the letter and felt happy. "But I don't want to do a blog," I told them. "That is too much work. It makes me tired just thinking about it."

"Yes, I think that's a good idea," my husband said.

"I don't think I could do that," I said.

I pondered the thought, though. Every morning, I write. Could I do this, I wondered. But no, I need to finish my novel, I told myself. I don't have time to write a blog. I reread the letter.

"She wants us to dance, Luke!" I said to my son who loves to swing dance. He laughed.

I tucked the letter into my suitcase for safekeeping and we continued with our day. The next morning, I typed it into my computer, cherishing the words and reflecting on their hopefulness.

I kept coming back to it from time to time, rereading and savoring the encouragement. I shared it with other people. I considered the words. They came out of me, but I didn't feel it was me writing. When I thought about it, I realized that over the past several years, I had actually been falling in love with the Earth. She started her letter telling me she loved me. What a gift to know we loved each other.

Although I've always enjoyed nature, I don't think I took time to really appreciate God's creation earlier in my life. For many years, I've noticed that spending time in nature rejuvenates me, and I started to realize that the trees actually give me oxygen, so physically, I am being restored.

By the time I received this first letter, I also sensed that my call included speaking for the Earth. So, to hear her say this directly and with such encouragement, warmed my heart to overflowing.

And the call to dance! I've been a little overweight for a long time, so I don't think people really want to see me dancing... and yet I yearn to dance. My husband and I love to dance together. I seek opportunities to dance. Years ago, I participated in a liturgical dance group. I've tried to get my son to teach me to swing dance. My husband and I like to go square dancing, contra dancing and we tried swing and waltzing lessons. That the Earth encouraged me to dance, also made me so happy inside.

She didn't "evolve us into consciousness over 4.7 billion years for us to sit like bumps on a log!" This makes me laugh with delight. She wants us to really enjoy our lives, to dance, to have fun, to be fully alive!

When I received this letter from the Earth, it spoke deeply to me, because my own path had gradually been awakening to listen and learn and love the Earth, to speak for the earth, to dance.

But still, I found myself wondering. Was that really the Earth, or was it just me? Certainly, it spoke of my life, but could the Earth write me a letter?

I looked for "not me" aspects of the letter. The idea of writing a blog was so not me. Although I have been developing a writing career and write daily, I just did not think I had the time and energy to do a blog.

And although I do what I can for the Earth, I also feel a sense of dread and concern that my actions won't make a difference. But, no, the Earth told me it's not too late and to continue to speak and join with others, working with others for her.

In the weeks after I received the letter, I kept sharing it with friends. I shared it with my spiritual director. She said, "Nancy, I do believe that the Earth is speaking to many people today. You must listen."

My friends and family encouraged me to do a blog. But a blog seemed a little too much for me to handle in my busy life. After a few weeks, I decided perhaps I could just receive more letters from the Earth. That would be simple. I would just listen and write. Maybe I could handle doing that. Yes, I decided I would try.

My 60th birthday came on the 4th of July, 2015. My sons came home from Seattle and Boston, my friends gathered at our house for an Earth Party. I thanked the Earth for my life, we wrote letters to Congress asking for action on climate change, we had an Earth art table, I danced with my husband, and we ate cake and ice cream.

And then, outside in our backyard on a beautiful summer day, surrounded by family, friends and flowers, I read out loud my original Letter from the Earth and announced my intention to continue to listen and write letters from the Earth.

My friends clapped. I laughed. Those gathered seemed to enjoy the letter. I didn't quite know what would happen next, but I made my public declaration, posted it on my website and would see what the Earth would tell me next.

A Letter from the Earth at Old Man's Cave – July, 2015

Introduction

      Just a few days later, while we entertained our son who came to Ohio from Seattle for my birthday, we discussed taking a day trip. We considered various possibilities. After some deliberation, he chose the southeastern Ohio mecca of Hocking Hills, where wooded trails and limestone cliffs lure many for hiking adventures, camping and journeys to enjoy the natural beauty throughout the year.
      Although the day trip was my idea, I found myself tired as we started off. My husband and I visited there for a weekend just a week earlier for our

30th wedding anniversary, so I hoped they would choose a different place, but still tried to be enthusiastic. Just driving down there takes over two hours.

When we arrived, we parked in the rather full lot at Hocking Hills State Park. And then, we made a beeline for Old Man's Cave, an unusual rock formation that draws thousands of visitors each year. Old Man's Cave is not really a cave, but a large overhanging rock, by a stream. The legendary "old man" actually resided there in the early 1900s. We headed down on the wooded path to the cave on this rather hot and humid July day.

Soon, we reached the bottom of the natural gorge, revealing a quite spectacular scene. A natural waterfall spills off nearby cliffs, cascading into the stream below. The overhanging cliff, creates a cool shelter on the stones above the water. On this warm day, people waded in the water under the falls, stood under the cliffs and were scattered along the trail.

My son wandered over to watch the water. My husband followed. But me? I just felt hot and tired. My shirt clung to my chest, I sweated, and I realized how much I needed a break. And so I took one. I lay down on the earth, appreciating the coolness there, putting my backpack under my head and actually went to sleep.

After a short nap, I felt refreshed for the rest of the day. We continued hiking, found some lunch and then went to rent boats at Lake Hope. My son chose a bike on top of a flat boat and began pedaling around the pristine, still waters. My husband and I picked a canoe. I sat in the back, steering and enjoying the late afternoon light shimmering on the water, feeling completely at peace as we paddled around the lake, taking in the cooling trees. It turned out to be a wonderful day after all, and we were all impressed, once again, with the natural beauty of Ohio.

A few days later, I felt the Earth wanted to talk to me about this experience, and so I took my hand to paper again. And then I received this second letter from the Earth.

The Letter

Dear Nancy,

Do you understand I want to connect with you?

You were tired that day at Old Man's Cave. You were hot. I know I was rather humid that day. But fortunately, you had the good sense to stop and lie down and what do you remember?

I think you can still feel the cool earth greeting I gave you. I am really very cool to touch, and your body connected with mine. I received you into my bosom. You felt me cooling you down, and then you went to sleep. When you woke up, you were refreshed, weren't you?

You humans rush about like little ants. You don't have to; you know? I gave you two legs, not wheels or wings, just legs. Slow down and rest and you will discover much more of my story.

That day, I told you to explore me. I want you to get out and around and enjoy me. Hiking is good, but stopping and observing is better. Sit, write, photograph, draw, paint. Absorb my reality and you will hear me more clearly.

At Old Man's Cave, you could get a sense of the eons of time that have led to where we are today. You saw huge stones. You could imagine the ancient sea, the earthquakes, the shifting plates, the erosion, the mighty forces that led to the environment now on my face. You stopped, and you appreciated the

evidence of millions of years of change.
You might feel small in comparison to my history, but know you are great. You humans are my pinnacle. Don't let you also become my demise.
Yes, you felt me crying. The waterfalls are refreshing, but also a spilling, a letting go, the way I cry.
Nancy, keep connecting with me. We have a sacred thing going here. Just show up. Listen. Observe. I will speak. You will find rest, refreshment and glimpses into my mystery.

I love you. - Gaia

My response

So, you see, it took me awhile to decide that I would welcome more letters from the Earth. After three months of haggling with the possibility and then announcing my intention to listen at my 60th birthday party, I opened myself to the Earth and this next letter came a few days later.
The Earth made me laugh. "Rushing around like little ants?" She definitely described me on most days. "I gave you two legs, not wings." I laughed again. I love the motif of flying. I want to fly. But the truth being said, I'm intended to be a grounded being. Yes.
The lesson of this letter is something that I'm still trying to absorb. I am often much too busy and I know it. I struggle to find an easier pace in life. This wonderful letter from the Earth gives me permission to slow down. I love it. I appreciate so much this message from the Earth.
And the Earth helps me appreciate the marks of time as I considered the unusual rock formations in the cave. I realize the billions of years leading to

landscapes of today. I realize my place in the natural world, the "pinnacle," she says. And I do feel like I am walking on very holy ground.

So, I felt rather delighted that the Earth cooled me off, refreshed me and then gave me a deeper sense of herself, calling me to slow down.

A Letter from the Earth at Lakeside – August, 2015

Introduction

At the end of July, I visited Lakeside, a Chautauqua on Lake Erie, a wonderful place I've loved since I was a little girl. The Chautauqua movement became popular in the late 1800s. The historians tell us that people arrived by boat and camped, later building Victorian cottages to provide a place of rest and restoration in the midst of summer. They were religious gatherings, but also included recreation and entertainment. Nowadays, we describe the Chautauqua as a place to nurture "mind, body and soul."

Lakeside, affiliated with the United Methodist Church, welcomes the annual conference of the church early in the summer, before the vacationers arrive. And so, as a child, we were treated to a vacation once a year while my dad (a United Methodist pastor) attended meetings. Later, my parents purchased a small cottage there for only $6,000 in the 1970s when the area experienced decline.

However, Lakeside rebounded in the 1980s and now that little cottage would sell for $150,000 or more. When I thought about buying a summer home there a few years ago, there were few houses under $200,000. It's become a vacation place for the wealthy, and it still provides a wonderful place for people of all ages.

A large auditorium provides nightly entertainment. The lakefront includes a dock for fishing, two swimming areas, one with a small beach for sand play, as well as a kiddie pool and fountains for the toddlers. Sailboats are available for rent. A pavilion above the pier provides Adirondack chairs and a cool place to sit and enjoy the view and water fun. Other offerings of this gated vacation land include educational sessions on a variety of timely topics, daily Bible Studies led by a Chaplain of the Week, religious services on Sunday, an arts and craft cottage, planned religious activities for the children, shuffleboard courts, miniature golf, and bicycles and golf carts to rent.

After my brothers and I started our families, we began to bring them to Lakeside for a family reunion every other summer. Our children enjoyed learning to sail together, swimming and riding their bikes along tree-lined, quiet streets, and engaging in evening family card parties, while their parents enjoyed the slower pace of summer in a friendly community that encourages relaxation.

On this particular summer, a friend and I signed up to teach photography at the Rhein Center for the Arts, to give us free entrance into the community for the week. For the first time, I visited without my family, but with my friend, another couple and also my husband for the weekends.

When I arrived, I hurried down to the long iconic pier, full of memories from childhood and beyond. I remembered my mom's ritual to always head out to the end of the pier to touch the flag pole when she arrived at Lakeside. I thought I would do that first. But as I walked under the pavilion and onto the dock, a sign stopped me cold, indicating that algal blooms were infesting the waters, so swimming and boating were not recommended. I walked out to touch the flagpole, and then went back to our cottage, heartbroken.

I stayed away from the lake most of the week. The water reopened twice during the week, only to close again. Between the farmers' runoff and warmer water temperatures from climate change, this northern Ohio playland and drinking water source is quickly becoming a dangerous container of bacteria.

However, the final morning, I spent my prayer time at the lake, something I would normally do every day of my week at Lakeside. This photographer's playland includes flowers lining the walking path, boats perched along the shore, rocks meeting waves, a scalloped pavilion with welcoming chairs, all providing excellent frames to capture the beauty of the sun rising over Lake Erie. I regretted not coming sooner.

So, on the very last day of my week, I finally made it down to photograph the sunrise, something I would normally do every day of my visit. And once I walked into the sun, capturing the beauty of the sunrise and the flowers and the water, my soul rejoiced in this experience of greeting day. There, I enjoyed the new gardens adorning the waterfront, providing ample opportunities for my camera-clicking soul. I walked by the pier, remembering my mother rushing to the end to circle the flag pole, her ritual for the first day of each visit to Lakeside. I walked by the sailboats lying on the water's edge, remembering when my sons and niece and nephew took lessons there one summer. I remembered laughing and doing water aerobics with milk jugs in the water with my dear cousin, Dave, no longer with us. So many memories clamor around this place for me. And on this day, new memories were made.

After my manic photoshoot, the sun lifted into a brilliant morning and I sat down to meditate. Every morning now, I sit into silence and give thanks for the gift of a new day. When I have an opportunity to sit by the water and watch the world waking up, I feel doubly grateful and mesmerized by creation. After my meditation, I began to journal and once again the Earth decided to speak.

The Letter

Dear Nancy,

I love you. I love the many delicate flowers you have photographed with my sunrise this morning. I love each person you interacted with this week. Do you understand that all of creation is an expression of my love and that you humans, my pinnacle, I call to love?

I know you are very sad about my problems. I am, too. And listen to the cacophony of Earth voices clamoring to call the people to awaken, to act, to rescue, to save.

You have heard my call. Thank you. Thank that husband of yours for his relentless efforts on my behalf. I know he has inspired you to do more.

The best you can do is to affirm the Earth care actions in others. Notice. Praise. Take delight.

Be aware of the cacophony. Hear the multitudes. Don't despair.

The lake will live again because of people like you and the Lakeside Environmental Stewardship Society (LESS).

Don't forget to always love and dance. I say Dance!

Love, Gaia, Your Creator

My response

Whew! This letter blew my socks off.

My week at Lakeside included avoidance of the iconic lakefront. I really did not want to face the problem of climate change during my vacation. I always went to Lakeside to rest and refresh my soul. I didn't want to mourn. I wanted to rejoice.

I have to admit that as I have begun to realize the devastating human impact on the planet, my first tendency is depression and a sense of overwhelming dread. And in the beginning of my awakening, I really didn't think I could do anything about it.

So what did the Earth have to say? "The best you can do is to affirm the Earth care actions of others." This message spoke so deeply to me. Not only to affirm, but to recognize the cacophony of voices clamoring in this day to speak for the Earth.

This letter made a believer of me. I truly began to believe that these letters came from a Source beyond me. I suspected that from the beginning, because I had no interest in being a blogger. And I felt the earth really communicating that day when she cooled me off and relaxed me at Old Man's Cave, but this letter seemed so concrete and helpful. It's something that continues to speak to me, again and again.

When she recommended I applaud my husband and to believe environmental groups will make a difference, words were planted deeply within my soul. That week at Lakeside, my husband and I met with the leader of the Lakeside Environment and Stewardship Society (LESS). I arranged this meeting to see if we could talk with them about our group, Citizens' Climate Lobby. As he shared the accomplishments of this group in this small community, he impressed us so much. They mobilized great work, instituted recycling, engaging in the problems with water of Lake Erie, and were praying and listening for more work. He agreed to schedule Steve to speak to the group in the future.

I try now to follow the Earth's advice. I have made a point to be grateful and express gratitude to those working for the earth. When I recognize the great people we work with in the CCL and how kind, creative and motivated they are to help create a livable planet, I feel so happy. I admire my husband even more and tell others. I appreciate the people working with us in Springfield. I also remember that Lake Erie had problems years ago, that were solved by careful concern. The Earth instilled hope that our efforts now could be successful again. And the Earth reminded me that I am not alone in my concern. I remembered reading that book *Blessed Unrest* a few years back. There are literally millions of grassroots efforts around the globe clamoring for change. No, I am not alone.

A Letter from the Earth While Praying with a Holy Icon-Late August, 2015

Introduction

For the past 6 years, I've been connected with the Shalem Institute for Spiritual Formation. This wonderful organization began over 40 years ago by Episcopal priest, Tilden Edwards, who felt a call to develop the contemplative life within the modern Christian church. Westernized Christianity often dwells in the realm of thoughts and mind, and lacks balance with the body and spirit. Tilden took a leap of faith back then, feeling this call, and he never looked back. For 40 years, the leaders of this organization have been teaching lay people and clergy on the path of Christian contemplation. For those looking for more depth in the spirit life, they offer a deep well and point the way to the value of the practice of silence.

I knew of them for years. I loved reading a book, *The Awakened Heart*, by one of their past leaders, Gerald May, and had a dream of bringing this sort of spirituality to my town. And, still, I don't think I really had any idea what they were about when I serendipitously signed up for their 18-month class on Leading Contemplative Small Groups and Retreats. That experience changed my life. Daily meditation, a requirement in the program, became a practice that transformed me from within. Their training led me into a depth of spirituality that keeps me coming back for more. I long to be a "contemplative evangelist" to share this wonder with others. I hear so many struggle with setting a discipline to meditate. For me, it's the favorite part of my day. I hate to miss it.

On the day I received this letter, I participated in a retreat led by two graduates of Shalem's program at Corpus Christi Center for Peace in Columbus, Ohio. We spent the morning praying with the senses, and then in the afternoon, they led us into the silence to pray with a Holy Icon. This meditative practice, we learn from the Eastern Christians. In the Russian orthodox churches, the walls of the cathedrals are filled with Holy Icons. A Holy Icon isn't a piece of art in the traditional sense, but something composed as part of a time of prayer. Those who make this form of art say that they receive them and don't take credit for the beautiful art.

I suppose the spiritual practice of writing a Holy Icon is quite similar to my experience of receiving and writing these letters from the earth. The earlier artists never signed their work, because they believe God wrote the picture through them. Usually, an important part of the paintings are the eyes that seem to follow you around the room.

There are several famous holy icons, such as the Sinai Jesus. I remember spending hours with that one on a silent retreat. But on this day, a rather strange icon called to me to pick it up and take it along with me to my place of meditation. This modern painting, by a brother of the cloth, Michael McGrath, was named appropriately "Star of the Sea."

At first, I didn't quite know what to make of her. Her eyes appeared closed, which made it difficult for me. I'm used to making eye contact with Holy Icons, but it seemed I could not. My eyes instead moved around her flowing garments, the waves, and the stars. After a while, however, it seemed that one of her eyes was closed and one open.

Holy Icons are considered "portals to God". And this one certainly opened a window for me that day, as I received yet another letter from the Earth, our Creator. Here is what she said.

The Letter

Dear Nancy,

Today, you realize there is much you don't know or understand about me. As you've been gazing at a representation of me as the "Star of the Sea" by Michael O'Neill McGrath, OSFS, you've had quite an experience of me, even though it's unclear and growing on you.

You see me as consciousness, as crown, as star of creation, birthing all of this planet which is body and also consciousness.

You see me with one eye closed and one eye open and you know the key to wakefulness is inner silence.

You see the heart centering, radiating light, the white light of love.

You see the mystery held in loving arms.

As you colored later, you saw your call as crown, too, of creation, to listen and to speak from your heart and to make peace from the wellspring of my peace.

You hear a call to listen to the polarities.

Here I call you.

My creatures find conflict. Help them listen. Help them find hope. Be light. Let your heart shine.

Love, Gaia, The Star of the Sea, Your Creator God

My Response

I love this message from the Earth that came that day. For I saw the "Star of the Sea" as God teaching me. The Earth once again reminded me of her role in birthing all of creation, then evolving us into consciousness to also be the crown of creation with her. Over time, I have come to cherish this idea that we are the consciousness of the Earth. Certainly, the Creator of our universe is pure consciousness, and thus we are made in God's image.

The dual eye situation taught me of the need for inner silence in order to be fully awake, which also really spoke to me. I see a gradual awakening among the people of the planet these days. And those who cultivate inner silence seem to be the most awake. It is so important for us all to awaken and begin to care for the earth.

The other thing about this letter that really led me deeper into my life was the call to listen to the polarities, to help others listen and to be a peacemaker. For over 20 years now, I've served as a mediator, a peacemaker. And always, my goal is to listen and help others be heard. That the Earth affirmed this vocation of mine really encouraged me. And that she encouraged me to embrace the polarities also totally moved me.

Has there ever been a time before now in which we as a country were so polarized politically that sometimes it seemed like more energy went into putting down those with whom we disagree than solving the great problems of our day? During the past eight years of our presidential cycle, the Republicans and Democrats have cooperated on very little legislation to move our country forward. I am as guilty as the rest of tending toward these divisive actions, although now I am learning to call for bipartisan solutions on climate change.

Has there ever been a time before when people seemed to be talking right past each other? Well, probably, but here we are again. It's hard not to fall into the trap of putting down those with whom we disagree. And it really seems that most politicians spend more time complaining about the other party than actually going about solving the great problems we face.

I believe here, the Earth called me to go beyond the "either/or" into the "both/and," which I know to be quite a challenging spiritual call. When I stand on sacred ground, everything illuminates before my eyes. Such was my experience that day.

A Letter from the Earth: Garden Party-September 13, 2015

Introduction

My friend, Chris, had been fighting ovarian cancer for 5 years. On her birthday in July, I gave her a coupon for each month so that we could do some special things and have a good time in the midst of the treatments and doctor visits. When I created a coupon for a Garden Party, I didn't really even know what I offered. I just thought it would be nice to do something in the backyard, while all the flowers were still blooming.

I don't think I have a green thumb, but I've been learning to grow things since we've lived in this house. We started a vegetable garden in the backyard shortly after moving in. I planted tulip and daffodil bulbs along the front walk, and always fill the narrow beds with bright annuals in May. A few years ago, I started what I call "The Mother's Garden" in the sunny front corner of our lot, to honor our gardening mothers who passed away in 2006. Then, my friend Naureen helped me develop a vision for the shady part of our backyard, and we filled pots with shade-tolerant blooms. I also created some pocket gardens in the corners of the yard and planted morning glories along the fence. When trees died, I've created additional gardens along a little sidewalk that extends out to the back of our lot which originally led to a barn.

Now the shaded part of our backyard is a beautiful place to be all summer long. My husband purchased a hammock for me. We have a couple Adirondack chairs, a round glass table and other plastic chairs which I scatter around the potted plants. Grass doesn't grow very well under the trees, but I hardly notice that anymore in this great space for conversation, meditation and a summer meal. I really love our shady, green and blooming backyard. When I made the coupon for Chris, I was thinking we could spend some time back there, hanging out with the flowers before they died back for the winter.

My friend Naureen not only can turn a boring landscape into a blooming masterpiece, but she also won flower arranging contests as young woman in her native Pakistan. When I invite her over during the summer months, she comes with a beautiful bouquet in hand. Perhaps she could teach us to do that, I thought. Wouldn't that be a wonderful activity for a garden party? I asked her, and she readily agreed. Naureen is also one of the most generous souls I know. She spends her work life teaching nursing students at the community college, going above and beyond to encourage them to strive for excellence in their studies, and later as nurses. She gave up her medical career as a doctor when she left Pakistan but continues to share her knowledge and so she did with us.

And also, in early September, the garden's bounty of fresh fruits and vegetables abound, so I thought I'd ask everyone to bring a salad, a drink and dessert. I created a little agenda for the day, which included a card game at the end. This particular group of friends loves to play our family tradition of "Oh Heck." We created a list of "refined exclamations" to use during the game, in our garden party attire. I suggested that the ladies wear hats, and the gents bow ties.

The weather cooperated for our Labor Day Garden Party that exceeded all my expectations. I set the backyard table with fine china and silver and a pretty tablecloth. We dined among the flowers and savored such delicious salads, herbal teas and fruits. It truly turned out to be a delightful afternoon. I turned Ricky Nelson's "Garden Party" on some speakers on the back porch to serenade our luncheon, and we all realized that we had been singing that song to ourselves as we prepared for the day. I took pictures of the event unfolding and later put the pictures to music, which you can view on YouTube if you wish at: *Labor Day Garden Party 2015.*

I told my friends to bring a vase. We cut flowers from my garden beds, and Naureen also brought additional flowers from her yard and a few from the store. After our lunch, we cleared off the table and she gave us our first flower arranging lesson. We learned that odd numbers are important. Include 1, 3, or 5 of each flower or green – never an even number she told us. We learned to start with the highest stem, 1½ times the height of the vase. And with those few rules of thumb, we began our flower art projects. So many possibilities and ways to arrange the beauty, we each soon developed a masterpiece, with a little tweaking and help from Naureen.

The next morning, the Earth wrote me this letter about our experience.

The Letter

Nancy, dear,

Yesterday, you came home to me and participated in an exquisite garden party. Surrounded by my beauty, you partook of my bounty and experienced the fullness of me, living with joy with your favorite people.

I noticed that you paused to consider the great variety and diversity of the plants and flowers in your yard. I noticed you savoring Chris' deliciously spiced brown and white bean salad with green celery, Naureen's colorful salsa of yellow corn, red tomatoes and peppers, green cilantro and black beans, the fruit kabobs of orange melon, red strawberry and yellow pineapple. I observed you enjoying the fresh mint and herbal teas from my leaves. And you inhaled that delightful new dish your husband created, potato tomato salad, and Karol's green lettuce salad with that Greek dressing you love and Holly's brussel sprout offering.

Do you pause every day to give thanks for the amazing offerings of earth? Do you realize how generous I am in sharing life with you?

Please return the favor. Be generous, please. You'll find it leading you into ever more abundant love.

Later, when Naureen became teacher, you began to notice the flowers and greenery more, didn't you? Flower arranging is such a noble art, taking my beauty and developing compositions that delight and astound. You watched your friends, mesmerized with the possibilities of Earth art, didn't you?

You each composed flower bouquets – delicate and blooming, arranged into artful display, delighting the eye and presenting me to brighten the day.

Did you hear Naureen say she always has fresh flowers in her kitchen and bathroom? A little bit of me, artfully arranged to keep always connected to me in the many mundane moments of her day.

Nancy, Nancy, Nancy. Do you see life is a precious gift to be savored? Enjoy your flowers. Enjoy feasts of my bounty. Enjoy your friends, my crowning glory. Slow down and be present.

I love you.

Your Creating Mother, Your Favorite Father, Word Alive in all of creation, Gaia God

My Response

Wow, the earth had me at hello on this one.

As Ricky Nelson sings, "We went to the garden party to reminisce with our old friends," and we had the time of our lives. The Garden Party turned out to be quite a spectacular event in my life, and I believe in the lives of my friends. This letter totally topped it off for me.

She called me to practice gratitude. I do, and I know I can do more. Gratitude evokes so many good feelings inside.

She called me to be generous, telling me it will lead me into abundant love. I am generous, but I know I can do more. Sometimes I hold on to tightly to what I have.

She told me to savor and enjoy my life, my friends, the food, and the flowers. I do, but so often, I eat without savoring. So often, I spend time with friends without really appreciating their gifts. So often, I forget to give more away. So many times, I forget to notice the flowers.

Did you notice that the Earth keeps giving herself different names when she signs her letters? In this letter, she uses "Your Favorite Father". That's the first time she referred to herself as a male! I appreciate the various names she uses, and that here she uses both "father" and "Word". Both of these terms are used in the Bible to refer to God.

Over the years in the Christian church, I've followed and engaged in the debate over the gender of God. Although most would agree that God transcends gender, within the Judeo-Christian circles, God seems to be considered decidedly male.

When people start to refer to God as "she", then some are concerned that you are crossing the bridge into the "pagan" religions where we encounter the Goddess. And yet even in the Bible, female words are used for God. "Ruah", the Hebrew word for "Spirit", is feminine. "El Shaddai", another Hebrew term for God, also means breast and mountain. Other biblical images of God include a mother hen, gathering her chicks under her wings, and a woman searching for a lost coin.

The Hindus have a hundred different representations of God. And while some Christians call these the "other gods" and "graven images" that are forbidden in the Bible, my Hindu friends have explained that these just express different aspects of the same one God. Sort of like the blind men exploring an elephant, don't you think? How would it be possible to categorize our Higher Power who created all of life and moves through all life with only one word?

In this letter, the Earth embraced my

experience while naming my joy and calling me to focus on what's most important. I felt so blessed.

A Letter from the Earth Concerning CultureFest- September 30, 2015

Introduction

For the past 19 years, part of my job in Human Relations for the City of Springfield has been to help put on CultureFest, an annual festival celebrating the diversity of our community. My coworkers and I in Community Development put a lot of time into coordinating this event.

In my life, I am drawn to people of other cultures. I enjoy learning about their rituals. I enjoy eating food of different ethnic and national origins. I draw truth and light from their spiritual traditions. Yes, long ago, I discovered that relating to people who are different from me enriches my life beyond imagining.

So when my boss asked me to come up with a plan to organize a festival to celebrate diversity in our town some 21 years ago, and told me, "Nancy, I think this is something you'd like to do," I quickly responded, "Yes!" I went back to my desk and started thinking about how we could pull people together to get the job done. We assembled a steering committee and began. Twenty years later, we're beginning to plan now for our 20th anniversary festival, and I still find my passion for this event, although my coworker and I, who do most of the work, also get rather worn out each year.

As CultureFest 2015 approached, I became sick the week before the event, but had to keep pushing through. I coordinated volunteers, trying to make sure we had coverage throughout setup, the various activities during the day and cleanup. I wrote announcements for the three stages. I arranged food for the volunteers and worked on last minute promotions. I made sure we pushed out as much information as possible on where to park, what would be happening, and inviting people to come on down. On the actual day of the event, I showed up and put in the 14 hours required from beginning to end, but I really didn't have the energy to dance, which saddened me. Several of the performers usually call up the audience to participate, and I particularly love these moments of CultureFest where I join the dance.

We've discovered over the years that it's really the dancing that makes this event so powerful. Of course, the food and music and hands-on activities for children, also contribute wonders, but to see people dressed in bright colors of native garb, dancing? I think that just makes people downright happy, me included.

CultureFest also provides a day of wonderful and colorful sights for avid amateur photographers like me. During CultureFest, I tend to traverse the City Hall Plaza nonstop, trying to capture each group on three stages, and also get shots of the people, the faces of the children, the food and vendors, the merchandise and the crafts and lessons.

No wonder I usually need a week to recuperate each year! After CultureFest, I take a break! I nurse my aching feet and sit down at the computer to relive the day through my pictures. During my time of recuperation after the 2015 CultureFest, I received this letter from the Earth.

The Letter

Dear Nancy,

You experienced me in my divine glory in the people gathered Saturday at CultureFest on the Springfield City Hall plaza. There, you see why I call you and all earthlings to dance. It's in your blood, yes?

The pinnacle of the day was that XClusive Dance Group who filled the plaza as they twirled to the Hip Hop music of our times. "All of Me," celebrating your hometown John Legend, and celebrating other creative muses – like LaJuan Dotts, Xclusive Creator, expressing Spirit in movement.

Next up, the Indian dancers splashed the plaza with color, sublime movements and fun. You delighted in the row of male turbaned heads watching their Sikh women twirling with dances of their homeland, sharing joy with all. So happy that they could celebrate and share their culture on the City Square.

And then you checked out the Egyptian Breeze

Belly Dancers gyrating in the CultureDance tent. Enjoying the beautiful women, noticing your local businessman, Jim Lagos, appreciating their gifts as did you.

Yes, this is the stuff of life that carries you all into joy. Dance! I say dance!

You might have been a little under the weather Saturday and couldn't dance yourself, but you smiled and laughed and appreciated the others. I hope you will really make more time in your life to dance. It's good for you, you know?

Then back to the dance tent later, I noticed you mesmerized by the smooth movements of the Urban Line Dancers, gently rotating out and embracing in, completely synced to one another, a hip-hop swing of mellow motions, expressing love with partners. Yes, I love to watch this, too.

And there you saw the Hula dancers clicking their sticks into a circle, swaying, moving, teaching the children to dance. And you photographed Shih Ming execute the long form of Tai Chi, moving effortlessly through space, moving Chi, moving in harmony, maintaining a healthy body, teaching you how to live.

And you enjoyed Mexico native, Beatriz Koehler, once again teaching the children to do the Mexican Hat Dance at CultureJam. They laughed. The girls quickly mastered twirling their skirts. The boys proudly donned the Mexican hats. The Mariachi Band smiled, watching the younger generation learning the ropes.

There at CultureFest, a cacophony of sound and music and silence united you all with common heartbeats of life. The African dancers featured their drummers and you felt that harmonizing pulse of life. Didn't you feel it moving them? Didn't you see it as they brought others up to dance along?

Project Jericho carried that beat along also. When you visited them in the CultureDance Tent, you saw most of the young bowed, and then one by one, they awakened into that rhythm of life, sitting up tall, joining the concert, deepening the sounds of this community of drummers, inviting you also into that joyful pulse of being alive.

Yes, Nancy, CultureFest is a very good thing. Keep it going. Keep the beat. Find ways to dance along. Take time to realize and appreciate the significance of this community celebration.

Thanks to you and to all of those making this happen. Thanks to all of those expressing the joy of life. Please thank them for me. This is the splendor of life; the meaning of the gift of life which I offer to you all.

Love, The Creating God of Earth

My Response

When I received this letter about CultureFest from the Earth, I felt so happy that she liked our event and that she loves the dance. Here, she underscores the importance of our event and expresses gratitude to all of those who make this day happen.

As I reread this letter, I notice she encourages me to focus on each dancing group. She calls me to pay attention. I went back through my pictures, looking for the details, and felt so rich with the outpouring of joy and expression shining out there.

And I really felt appreciated for the work I do. That was so kind of the Earth to thank me and the many others who make the event possible. We do work very hard to make the event successful. What a gift for her to express this gratitude to me and all of the people that make it happen.

Do you see how helpful these letters are to me personally? Gaia seems to be quite a happy and loving spirit and her wisdom comes to me in many ways through her letters. As I rested and regathered my strength after CultureFest, I felt myself smiling deep inside, knowing that I would enjoy organizing the next year's event even more, after receiving her encouragement and affirmation.

A Letter from the Earth Concerning Travels in Ireland- October 19, 2015

Introduction

Ever since a man asked me if I am Irish when I was a little girl, I have been intrigued with Ireland. When I asked my mother if I'm Irish, she said, "No, honey, you're not Irish." But when I researched my family tree in college, I discovered my maternal grandfather's mother was Irish. I celebrated by going to an Irish pub, having some beer and dancing and later that year, finding an Irish boyfriend for a while.

But the last few years, as my spiritual path deepened, I felt drawn to learn more about Celtic spirituality. In working at building contemplative offerings in our town, a couple years ago, we invited Carl McColman, a contemplative writer and retreat leader from Atlanta, a lay Cistercian of Irish descent. One of Carl's sessions was an introduction to Celtic Spirituality. I began to learn about how the form of Christianity in Ireland was quite different than most other places. Because the Romans didn't conquer Ireland, when St. Patrick arrived on the Emerald Isle, he encountered the Celtic spiritual traditions, rooted in the earth. And therefore, Christianity developed there with a close kinship with the Earth. The Celtic cross includes the circle of life.

Carl asked me to consider arranging a contemplative pilgrimage to Ireland with him as our leader. I started to explore this possibility, when my husband agreed to go there with me for our 30th anniversary. But, it was difficult to navigate this process, and eventually, I decided just to plan the trip for us. Nevertheless, I hoped to learn more about their deep spiritual tradition.

In early October, 2015, right after CultureFest, my husband and I took our 30th anniversary adventure to Ireland. I planned quite an ambitious one-week trip, knowing it might be the only time in my life to visit the Emerald Isle. My husband and I rented a car for a whirlwind tour, trying to take in the popular tourist sites. We started in Dublin with a hop-on, hop-off bus to travel around the city, visiting Trinity College and the Artist's Museum. We took a bus tour south to the Wicklow Mountains and the Glendalough Monastery. Then we headed up to Newgrange, followed by two nights on the west coast first in the little fishing town of Kinvarra, and later on the southwest Dingle Peninsula, where I happily played my fiddle in an Irish pub, crossing that off my bucket list.

At the beautiful Cliffs of Moher on the west coast, I took time to explore their indoors exhibits. I pushed buttons on a display of the earth that talked about our changing climate. When they said that that Dublin, Galway and Cork might all be underwater in 150 years, I stopped in my tracks. Ireland is an island. The ice caps at the poles are melting. Sea level is rising. I know this. I know the predictions. In Miami, Florida, a city at sea level, the salt water is already starting to find its way into the ground water. But there on this happy day, exploring the magical island, this forecast floored me. I pushed the button again and called my husband over to look.

After exploring western Ireland, we headed east for a night at Blarney and then back up toward Dublin. Although we visited two ancient monasteries, for the most part, it seemed that Ireland for tourists does not provide an introduction to Celtic spirituality. The last night when we stayed with a young American family, they told us they knew more people into Celtic spirituality in the USA than they encountered in Ireland. They said that there has been a mass exodus from the Catholic Church in recent years following the sex scandals, and the country is quickly becoming secularized.

The last day, however, we also visited a retreat center where the nuns of the St. Brigid order are keeping the ancient Celtic tradition alive deep in the heart of their Christian spiritual practice. St. Brigid, who started an order of nuns, near the time of St. Patrick, incorporated the ancient stories of Brigid, an Earth goddess. Sister Mary greeted us warmly and spoke of their friend John O'Donohue, a Celtic spirituality writer. She said the Dalai Lama visited them, and Brian Swimme, an author I enjoy. Their modern retreat center uses no fossil fuels and works to develop an earth-centered contemplative spirituality for travelers and locals. There, I visited St. Brigid's well. Wells are considered holy places in the Celtic tradition. Although I didn't get quite as much Celtic spirituality in Ireland as I hoped, meeting Sister Mary made me smile and she pointed me to teachers and I continue to learn.

When I returned home, I received yet another letter from the Earth concerning this trip.

The Letter

Dear Nancy,

Thank you for visiting my Emerald Isle of Ireland, a special place of mine. You Americans find it entrancing and enchanted... and so do I. Her history overflows with people deeply connected to me.

Weren't you amazed with the ingenuity of these prehistoric builders of Newgrange who created that magnificent waterproof building out of stone? That 5,000 years later, the sun still illuminates its ceremonial center three days of the year at the winter solstice? Moving rocks weighing tons, building a still water-tight rock dome, honoring and understanding the seasons and changing sun? Yes, those early people paid attention to me.

Weren't you mesmerized by the Druid Forest at Blarney Castle where you saw their huge holy stones, cascading falls, rambling trees, shamrocks and could feel the magic of nature? Most of nature has this feel, if you really pay attention. The Druids felt the mystery of it all and I think you did, too, that day.

Didn't you love the 40 shades of green in rambling fields divided by stone fences, the coast lands, the beautiful Cliffs of Moher, the Dingle Peninsula taking you closest to your son in Boston, and the Wicklow Mountains south of Dublin? So much of the variety of my earth is displayed wonderfully on this small island.

And weren't you totally delighted to meet Sr. Mary at the Solas Bhride Center for Spirituality and Hermitage at Kildare? Isn't their new green building totally cool, not using fossil fuels for heating and cooling, providing a fit tribute to St. Brigid, who shares a deep spiritual tradition before Christianity came to Ireland? You walked to St. Brigid's Well and felt that connection to earth, to the wellspring of all life.

And everywhere, you saw the Celtic crosses – at the Glendalough and Clonmacnoise monastery ruins where monks kept hope alive, merging scholarship and church and caring for Earth. The Celtic cross incorporates both the circle of life as well as suffering love, so important for the people of my creation.

Yes, Ireland is quite a place to learn. And I know you are very concerned about its future, and the future of our planet. That was very sobering to read the climate change display at the Cliffs of Moher stating that in 150 years, Galway, Cork and Dublin might all be underwater.

Don't stop your work on climate change. You are part of a wonderful organization, this Citizens' Climate Lobby. The Paris Talks are coming up. Keep organizing. Keep speaking. Keep encouraging others to get involved. And Nancy, I like your monthly pledge website.

Thank you for taking time to spend your resources to explore and understand me better. I think it was a great learning and loving experience. Don't you?

Love,
Your Mother who created Earth, Your God

My Response

When I received this letter from Gaia, I felt happy to know she appreciated the Celtic spiritual traditions. Sometimes, I find fellow Christians dismissing the earlier peoples who lived much closer to the Earth. When I stood in the center of the ceremonial building at Newgrange, created over 5,000 years ago by prehistoric peoples and heard how it lines up with the sun at the winter solstice three days each year, I felt honored to be in this sacred space, celebrating the mystery of the seasons.

I also appreciated the Earth's words here on climate change. When you start to become aware of the grave danger of climate change, you start to wonder why it's so hard to convince our government to take action. When you read the science and quit listening to propaganda that tries to say there is no problem, you can become quite alarmed. It often feels like there's an elephant in the room. And sometimes I think perhaps I'm over-reacting. But no, the Earth tells me I'm not. I still shudder when I think about that display at the Cliffs of Moher.

When I received this letter from the Earth, I also appreciated that the Earth affirmed the Citizens' Climate Lobby (CCL) to which I belong. I love this group of dedicated people determined to convince our government to take action before it's too late. They do it by building relationships, affirming legislators, and being infinitely positive, creative and hopeful. They have doubled in number every year for eight years and their reach is extending. In the past year, 11 Republican Congress members have signed on to a resolution to take action on climate change. Four Republican Senators have formed a group to consider climate action. Most recently, Democratic and Republican Congress members from Florida have formed a bipartisan caucus on climate change and will add two members at a time, from both political parties. CCL is slowly making headway. They give me great hope, and so do these Letters from the Earth. I am most grateful to them both.

As part of my work with Citizens' Climate Lobby, last year, I started a website for Ohioans to take a monthly pledge to write a letter each month to legislators about climate change. It's been slow to catch on, but I've been excited about this way to make it easy for people to speak up on a regular basis. Each month, I post an action, based on the recommendations from our international organization. When the Earth told me here that she liked my website, I laughed and beamed deep within. That she noticed meant a lot to me. And that she tells me to keep working, speaking up and organizing, also encourages me.

Finally, here she tells me that she's glad I went to Ireland to explore more of creation. Do you remember she told me in the second letter to get out and explore? I learn so much when I have opportunities to travel, and I love that she encourages me to take adventures!

A Letter from the Earth about the Great Coming Together- December 6, 2015

Introduction

Last summer, the Pope published an encyclical on the Earth. On a beautiful October day, my husband and I went to Bergamo, a retreat center in Kettering, Ohio, where we received a teaching about the encyclical from a University of Dayton professor as part of a fall day of retreat. This Catholic center owned and operated by the Marianists and connected with the University of Dayton, includes an Environmental Center. One of their environmental projects is to return their land to its original prairie. After the morning teaching, we joined a nature walk with a biologist who explained the transformation of their nature preserve. At the end of the day, we participated in a percussion rendering of the encyclical with a local musician, using a combination of musical instruments to respond to the words of darkness and light in the encyclical. The day developed within me a deep appreciation for this encyclical of Pope Francis, entitled *Laudate Si*, which means "All Praise to You".

If you haven't read the Pope's encyclical on the Earth, I highly recommend it. It's an incredibly sacred and amazing treatise. I'm not Catholic, but wow! The Pope is so connected to the Earth; he took the name Francis when he became Pope. You know St. Francis? He's the one who preached to the birds and the animals, and wrote "Brother Moon, Sister Sky." In the encyclical, the Pope suggests that we need to find new ways to think about the created world, that we need new ways to relate to the Earth.

As a Christian, I have always been taught that we are "stewards" of the Earth, which implies a relationship of caretaking. This sort of thinking may focus on the idea that God put us in charge and we can use things for our benefit, or it may also focus on our responsibility not to misuse the resources, damaging the creation. What I didn't realize until listening to the Catholic professor interpret the encyclical that day, is that this sort of thinking evolved during the time of Henry the VIII when as King of England, he took over the monasteries of England and Ireland. He shut them down as centers of spirituality and learning to use them for his own purposes, amassing their wealth, especially the land they owned. And then he chose people to be "stewards" over his stolen lands to run them for his own benefit. After touring Ireland and learning about how the monasteries were holding the light of both learning and faith during the dark ages, this act of the King seemed quite brutal. I no longer see the term "steward" in a positive light.

Instead, the Pope recommends that we begin to realize that we are a part of creation, not in charge, but one aspect of creation. He suggests we might use the image of family, as St. Francis did. Our brother, the moon, our sister, the sun. Consider mutuality rather than stewardship. He also recommends that we approach the earth contemplatively. He says, "The universe unfolds in God, who fills it completely. Hence, there is a mystical meaning to be found in a leaf, in a mountain trail, in a dewdrop, in a poor person's face. The ideal is not only to pass from the exterior to the interior to discover the action of God in the soul, but also to discover God in all things." And much of the encyclical is calling us to change our way of life to begin to care for the Earth, addressing climate change, and changing destructive economic practices.

The words of the Pope, the interpretation of the Catholic educator, and how this synchronizes with my own awakening is reflected in this most recent letter I received from the Earth.

The Letter

Dear Nancy,

So you like our new Pope? He speaks for me so eloquently, awakening the people, calling them to see divinity in me. He calls you to see the Earth as part of your family and to realize you are all a part of this spectacular creation. Yes, you like this. You love that he calls the people to approach the Earth lovingly, as his namesake St. Francis did years ago.

What you hear from him, you have been learning also. When you contemplate the birds, a tree, the landscape, you hear God's Word revealed. All of these living beauties call you to understand the miracle of life, don't they?

Do you see the great joining at this point in human history? In spite of the wars and degradation of me, so many are awakening in this time, calling others to awake also.

So celebrate our Pope. Celebrate the Marianists who call people to care for earth at their center in Kettering. Celebrate your Shalem Institute for Spiritual Formation who helped in your own awakening. Celebrate Oprah Winfrey and Deepak Chopra. Celebrate, Nancy, that in all of these ways, there is a great coming together during this time.

Consider what you've read. Remember when you first read Judy Cannato's *Radical Amazement* and *Field of Compassion*? Remember *Spiritual Ecology: The Cry of the Earth*? Remember those teaching Lectio Divina with the earth? Remember Brian Swimme's *The Hidden Heart of Cosmos*?

Celebrate. Name this great coming together and let your voice join theirs. Sing! Don't be silent now.

Call others to awaken and dance and live the miracle. Go now and make disciples. I call you.

Be awake. Dance. Speak. Call. Love.

Love, Gaia God

My Response

Here the Earth tells me, "Celebrate. Name this great coming together and let your voice join theirs. Sing! Don't be silent now. Call others to awaken and dance and live the miracle. Go now and make disciples. I call you."

I love that the Earth recognizes the Pope. I find

many Catholic and non-Catholic friends are excited about Pope Francis and his concern for the Earth.

And She doesn't stop there. She also goes on to recognize the many other organizations and books speaking for the Earth. Without skipping a breath, she lauds the Marianists, who have been preaching and caring for the environment in Ohio for a very long time. This directive feels wonderful and so challenging at the same time.

As I write this, I'm working with my writing coach, Kathie Giorgio, to develop the Letters from the Earth into a book so I can share them with more people. So, you must know that I am taking the Earth very seriously when she tells me to speak up. And Kathie really thinks that you need to hear how the letters affect me as part of the book. So here I am, showing up to explain, and I find that this process helps me do exactly what the Earth asks of me. Sort of gives me goosebumps! Do you feel it, too?

The Earth also mentions that when we encounter her contemplatively by focusing on a bird, a tree or landscape, we hear God's word revealed. Some call this "Opening the Holy Book of Nature." As I described earlier, some contemplatives recommend practicing "Lectio Divina" (Divine Reading) of God's Word in nature. This process, originally developed by Ignatius of Loyola as a way to read the Bible meditatively, has been adapted to read the Earth. I love to do this. God teaches me so much when I take time to listen to creation.

And here, the Earth calls to attention some of my teachers. The Shalem Institute for Spiritual Formation is a wonderful nonprofit that has been the leader in teaching contemplative practices to the church for over 40 years now. They train lay people and clergy in Christian meditation, leading contemplative small groups and retreats and spiritual direction. My spiritual director, Loretta Farmer, who trained with them, once told me, "It was the best educational experience of my life." I would say that taking an 18-month class with them changed my life in ways that I am still only beginning to realize. And I believe that because of my meditation practice that they encouraged, I have quieted myself enough to be able to receive these Letters from the Earth.

    The books the Earth mentions in this letter have been transformative for me as well. Judy Cannato, a lay Catholic woman, wrote two wonderful books about the Earth and encourages us to consider it contemplatively. In *Radical Amazement*, she focuses on new scientific learnings about the cosmos, making them understandable with directions for further contemplation and discussion. In *Field of Compassion*, she explains the inner workings of all life. The field of compassion she describes at the center of this working, which is encountered through meditation, she believes now is helping us develop the competencies we need to move forward together. In *Spiritual Ecology: The Cry of the Earth*, Llewellyn Vaughan-Lee draws together a collection of essays from most of the world's spiritual traditions, who all bring a message that the Earth is crying out to us and that we must listen and change our ways before it's too late. Brian Swimme, in *The Hidden Heart of Cosmos,* describes the miracle of the history of the development of our Earth, which transformed him from an atheist into a believer, and he goes on to explain that the source of our great depression and drug culture is in large part from our focus on "dead" things in a materialistic culture. He calls us to reconnect with creation. Sister Mary, whom I met in Ireland, told me Brian Swimme also visited her retreat center.

    Yes, I believe the Earth is correct about the

Great Coming Together, and I appreciate her reminding me of all the good writing and amazing people speaking up and working for positive change who give me hope.

And then at the end of this letter, she again gives me a string of positive directives that make me so happy! She calls me to celebrate, sing, dance, love and join in this great coming together by lifting my voice. And so here I am, writing my responses to her letters. Are you falling in love with her like me?

A letter from the Earth on Christmas Day 2015

Introduction

The month of December here in Springfield, Ohio, was unseasonably warm. During the week of Christmas, we received torrential downpours, while elsewhere in the USA, flooding and tornadoes created yuletide nightmares. On Christmas Day, I went out for a walk in my neighborhood. I started down our front sidewalk and there, I saw my daffodils pushing up through the brown earth. The daffodils? They usually come up in March or April, not December. I went back in to get my camera, took some pictures and continued on my walk, during which I saw one man mowing the grass. I photographed decorative snowmen on the walk, but no real snow.

When the daffodils were up on Christmas Day, I felt rather disturbed. We live in a very surreal time. While the climate is changing, and the earth is heating up, there is a bubble of denial and confusion created by the fossil fuel industry's PR machine.

Although I know climate change is very real and that we humans are causing it, I want to believe it's not true. I'd like to throw my hat into the ring of the deniers. I'd like to say it's okay for the capitalists to continue to take and pollute whatever they want and release as much carbon into the air as needed for our comfort and production. I wish it were really okay for the humans to use up the Earth without check. Unfortunately, I know it's not.

As Christians here in the United States of America, we feel we have been blessed. There is quite a mythology around this blessedness which often blinds us to what we are actually doing. We have undoubtedly had an incredible run here on this continent with the great expansion, the Industrial Revolution, the technological age, an amazing democracy. Yet, we have had this run at the expense of other people, not at all in our great tenet to love our neighbors as ourselves.

We make up about 5% of the world's population but use 25% of the world's energy supply. We drive 1/3 of the world's cars. We acquired our land by killing off the Native Americans and then enslaving Africans. Now we outsource our production to developing countries where children make our clothing in sweatshops and our electronics are made in factories where people are paid pennies for their day's labor. Our politicians get elected for their pro-LIfe stance, while they are being bankrolled by the fossil fuel magnates who choose growing their billions ahead of the future of the planet. We're not just talking about unborn babies here; we're talking about the end of the human species.

And so, there's something about the daffodils on Christmas Day which really speaks to me. It's hard for me to sing "Joy to the World" when I consider the daffodils. But then that day, I came back in from my Yule walk, I paused to listen and received this, yet another letter of encouragement from the Earth.

The Letter

Dear Nancy,

Don't cry. Things are changing, always changing. This is life.

You walked out to visit me on Christmas Day and right outside your front door, you noticed the daffodils are coming up already. You're not used to this happening in December, are you? Just after winter begins, there with the solstice, you see the ground warming as if winter passed and spring began. That's change for you.

You see, I've been here already for several billion years. I've gone through many changes and I continue that way. Your husband tells you this frequently, and you know it's true. I will outlive you humans. You depend on me, but I don't really need you.

So, don't cry. You took pictures of all the snowmen figurines and flags, but the real thing isn't around this year. Instead, you have rain, sixty-degree weather and you're wondering what is coming next.

Let go and live in the moment, Nancy. You are trying to raise awareness about climate change and what you humans are doing with your fossil fuels. That's good. Keep it up, but don't give in to despair.

I keep telling you to dance, and I'm not making it up. I really do want you to celebrate this life you have. In a moment, it comes, and in a moment, it goes, and now is the time to live.

So dance, celebrate, laugh, be happy and share the Christmas daffodils. That's good. Keep speaking up for you, for me, for us. I love you. I love them all.

Love,
Your Mother, your Earth, your God

My Response

So, I'm feeling down on Christmas Day, but then, I get this letter from the Earth. And what does she say? "Enjoy! Live in the moment. Dance. Laugh. Be happy. Don't give in to despair. Speak."

The ultimate Christmas gift, really – a gift from God, this letter.

I mean, what do you think God is feeling about now? If you think of our Supreme Being creating a universe and setting this creation into motion. If you imagine waiting 4.7 billion years for humans to emerge to offer her company. And then She must watch the humans destroy creation with their unbridled greed? How must that feel? And yet, here is God telling me to enjoy life. Reminding me it won't last forever. "Live now, Nancy," she says.

I know I was very blessed to be born in 1955. I've had a very good life, considering the life of other humans who have lived on this planet. I know that life for me can't get much better. I'm concerned that life is about to get very difficult for many, and perhaps, me, too because of climate change.

So yes, this was my Christmas gift from God – a message to enjoy the moment and instructions to accept change. I know that both of these practices are keys to living a good life, in the midst of whatever comes my way. What do they say? It's not about what happens, but how you respond that makes all the difference.

Thank you, God.

A Letter from the Earth about the Darkness in the Winter- January 11, 2016

Introduction

    I've started worshipping the sun more as I age –appreciating the goodness I feel on a bright day. Even in the winter, the sun warms my skin on such days. My eyes need more light to see as I age. I realize I don't spend much time appreciating the darkness in my life.

    As the days grow longer during winter months, I hate that the sky starts to darken as soon as I leave work, and that the sun barely rises before I go back to the grind. I spend most of my daylight hours in the City building and I miss the evening walks I enjoy during the other times of the year. As a woman, I usually feel unsafe walking after dark.

Many people abhor the long nights of winter and they even cause depression for some. I remember once when I helped my friend from Florida who was shopping for an apartment in Iowa for her last year of law school. I discovered an inexpensive basement apartment for her. Financially, yes, a great deal, but for her, the darkness in the basement brought sadness, compounded by the long nights of winter. She suffers from seasonal affective disorder. I know others like this. Although I am fortunate that I don't have this problem, I do prefer a long sunny day to a short cloudy one.

One January morning, I rose early, lit a candle, letting it illuminate the darkness during my time of meditation. Then, I turned on the lamp by my chair to journal. I always begin with some words of gratitude. Then I consider ways I experienced God in the past day. I write some prayers of petition, and then I just write whatever I'm thinking about, working out issues of my life and often gaining inspiration. After writing for a while, I sensed the Earth wanted to talk to me. As I listened, this letter started spilling out across the pages of my journal.

The Letter

Dear Nancy,

You walk through the darkness at this time of year. The longest day has past now, and yet the dark lingers in the morning. You wake to pitch black skies and by the time you come home from work, darkness once again descends upon my landscape.

In your houses now, you have lights and barely experience that darkness. Take some time to go outside at night, Nancy. Let the darkness permeate your consciousness. Let that fecund reality settle into your psyche.

In many of your spiritual traditions, you worship the light. And light is obviously very important, but much of creation happens in total darkness. Think of the beginning of human life. The encounter of the sperm and egg? Total darkness. That darkness is the incubator for all of life. The fetus exists in darkness for months, slowly evolving into a functioning body.

Not only the darkness, but also the coldness that settles into earth at this season is important for nature. The animals, the trees, the ground all get a break. Harmful insects die, the trees go within, your annuals disappear, but your perennials hold life carefully within their roots and little stems, waiting for spring to wake them up again.

And you, too, need this break. As much as you humans complain about the cold, you also like the excuse to spend more time indoors, cuddling up with a book and a blanket, or watching TV. You enjoy your comfortable beds. You enjoy lighting candles and hibernating a bit yourselves at winter.

I created life out of this darkness. And now your scientists realize that 95% of all life is dark space and dark matter, of which they really know very little. Ah, Nancy, that is the mystery which I continue to unravel.

I hope a day never goes by when you forget to marvel at this created world. The place of earth is one of my crowning glories among the galaxies of life. Take time to notice the darkness.

The Christmas cactus as you call it can only bloom when it has those long nights. Much of life requires this darkness in other ways. Humans need the darkness of sleep for rejuvenation.

So, Nancy, when you consider this winter time, celebrate the darkness and be grateful for the long nights that are important to life on your planet.

And I encourage you to go out into the night and early morning darkness and experience it more fully.

With much love,
Your ever designing, ever creating, Gaia God

My Response

Once again, I receive the letter and respond, "Wow! I never thought of it that way, Gaia!' Here, the Earth helped me think of this in new light, or should I say in new darkness? Since I started receiving letters from the Earth, I've been learning to appreciate aspects of creation I usually dislike.

And yet, I do appreciate those little blinders I have to put over my eyes when I'm trying to sleep in a car or an airplane. When my eyes are totally deprived of light, I feel my body relax and sleep comes more easily. I totally appreciate the darkness in those times.

And I can remember and appreciate the utter stillness of walking at night in the country. Far from city lights, the stars and the moon shine brighter. I have a sense of that awesome darkness which contains us all, and I feel such inner peace in those moments.

And then the Earth brings up this dark space and dark matter issue in this letter.

We live in the scientific age when we think there is an explanation for everything. And yet – now as the scientists begin to consider the universe and the infinite galaxies, they find they really know only about 5% of all that is.

If you haven't learned about the mysteries inherent in the universe, take some time to learn. Did you know that the universe is expanding at an accelerating rate? In 1998, the Hubble telescope began to open new understanding to astronomers. At one point, they decided to direct it toward what appeared to be empty space, and there they began to discover infinite galaxies. Based on the pictures they accumulated and the wonders they observed, they now tell us that 68% of the universe is composed of dark space and 27% made up of dark matter. And they really don't understand either of these phenomena. They know more about what they are not than what they are. Check out the NASA website for more information on their discoveries. (http://science.nasa.gov/astrophysics/focus-areas/what-is-dark-energy/)

And this is why I'm learning to sit into the silence. I'm learning to appreciate that empty dark space of mystery. When I close my eyes and release my thoughts into the dark chasm of life, I am catapulted into realms I've never experienced before, which illuminate the rest of my day.

I remember a poem I wrote, trying to express this, as I began to first learn the Universe Story in that Ecospirituality class I attended a few years ago. I considered that my daily practice replicates the Hubble telescope pointed on seemingly empty space. And so the poem connected that dark space to my meditation practice. And this is a truth I've been considering ever since. When I remember this poem, I realize God has been teaching me to appreciate the darkness for a while now.

Entering the silence

I am learning to sit.
Some days it's hard.
Some days it's easy.

I am learning to listen for God.
Some days I hear nothing.
Some days the love washes over me into joy.

I am learning that we are all connected.
Some days I still feel solitary.
Some days I realize that 10,000 others join me every moment.

I am opening to awareness deep within me.
Some days I feel empty.
Some days I feel that pulsating reality bringing life.

I keep thinking about the courage of the Hubble scientists.
Some days posed on emptiness in the sky.
Some days to realize the darkness contained infinite galaxies.

I keep thinking if I have the courage to sit in silence.
Some days I will focus on that emptiness, too.
Some days I will realize the web of stars and relationship hold us all.

3/15/11 Nancy Flinchbaugh

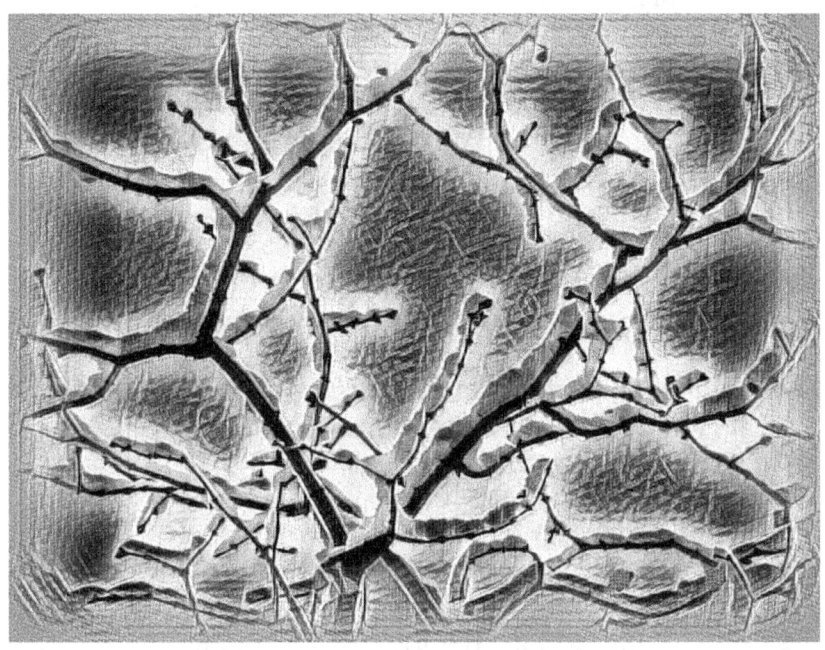

A Letter from the Earth about the Cold-January 14, 2016

Introduction

Ah, the cold!
In my twenties, I moved to San Antonio, Texas. And then for eleven years, I enjoyed mild winters and endured horrendously hot summers. When I moved back to Ohio to be with my parents in their later years, I found myself so happy to be back in the temperate zone.

Autumn, my favorite season, barely happened in San Antonio. Sometime in October, the first norther would roll in and then the temperature would start dropping below 77 degrees at night, bringing welcome relief from the scorching heat, but not much in the way of changing leaves or crisp nights. In order to see the leaves change, we would make a pilgrimage to Lost Maples State Park, northwest of San Antonio.

But then there's also winter in Ohio. My husband, raised

in Dallas, still grumbles about this time of year. He says give him heat any day, but the cold? No! Do our bodies become acclimated to the climate of our childhood? He likes the heat, and I prefer the mild summers and cooler weather. Or genetically are we predisposed to certain climate preferences? I'm not sure.

Certainly many northerners flee the cold in the winter, even if they have lived in the North for their entire lives. I love to escape to the beach. Retired people who have the resources often migrate south for the winter or move entirely to avoid the snow.

In Ohio, winter takes its time coming upon us. Sometimes we don't even get snow until December. So, by mid-January, the cold starts to become oppressive. I find myself longing for a warm, sunny day. On these cold winter mornings, I keep my pajamas on for my meditation. I snuggle under two blankets, crank up the thermostat, and sit close to our electric fireplace. I call the cat to sit on my lap as I deal with the frigid morning. It was a morning like this that the Earth wrote me the following letter.

The Letter

Dear Nancy,

Winter has come to Ohio. You breathe in fresh, crisp air and feel my refreshment. You snuggle under warm blankets, yet enjoy the cool air in your nostrils. Snow blankets the land. Ice forms on the trees.

You see the dormant land coated with beauty. You like what you see. Mesmerized, you walk into a new season that I've created for you. Quite wonderful, if I might say so myself!

You humans complain about the cold, and I know too much of it can be a very bad thing for you. This is true. And also, Nancy, the cold is so important to your ecosystem. In the mountains, snow creates a water supply for the warmer months. In the temperate zone, cold puts many bugs and pests to sleep and prevents other diseases from taking hold on the population. At the poles, the cold keeps your oceans stable and land masses exposed, not to mention providing home to those cute penguins and lumbering polar bears. It's all good, Nancy.

I've noticed you savoring cold this January, when you thought it might not come this year. And so now, I feel you welcoming cold a little more than usual. I've noticed that about you humans.

Sometimes it takes loss, or fear of loss, to help you truly appreciate the goodness of aspects of creation. I sense in you a gradual awakening to me over the past five years. And that is good. I enjoy your awakening into full reverence for the Earth.

So once again, I must tell you, Nancy, don't be dismayed. I much more hope you will be mesmerized and call your people to celebrate, care for the Earth, to dance, to speak out, to love, to realize this incredible miraculous planet in which you live, which is so very holy. That Pope Francis of mine got it right. Join him. Join all the voices, Nancy, all those speaking up, listening to me.

Don't be dismayed. Be mesmerized.
Dance. Laugh. Love.
I love you.

Your Gaia God

My Response

So true, dear Earth, we often don't savor what we have, until it's gone.

I think most people can appreciate the beauty of the newly fallen snow. And many of us still can capture a little of that childlike wonder and exuberance that takes us out to have fun in the icy blanket, making snow figures, snow angels, snow balls and snow tracks. But before I received this letter, I didn't quite realize how good and important to us this cold can be.

As the earth heats up, it seems quite often now the news brings reports of new mosquito-borne diseases. Lyme disease spreads, now deformed fetuses from a virus, increasing malaria. We need the long months of cold to limit these problems.

So, after daffodils on Christmas Day, I did really welcome the snowfall this year in January. And now I not only appreciate the beauty and the fun, but also the helpfulness of the cold and snow in winter.

A Letter from the Earth at the Beach-January 18, 2016

Introduction

As I've aged, I've learned to take care of myself more and more. I know I need breaks, reflection, exercise, laughter and vacation to keep me engaged fully in my life.

I suppose I'm also fortunate in that way, that I have the resources to take breaks. My husband and I live fairly frugally. We bought an inexpensive house and paid it off quickly. We buy our cars with cash, which saves quite a bit on interest. And so, we do have money to take vacations. And when we travel, we economize, often visiting people we know or finding other low-cost ways to enjoy the sights. When we went to Ireland last October, a coworker asked me, somewhat baffled, "How do you have enough money to do that?"

So many people live paycheck to paycheck. We haven't

needed to balance our checkbook for years, although when we quit for a while, our credit union started paying someone else's mortgage from our checking account and we didn't figure that out for six months. Now we do keep an eye on that. We're not wealthy by any means, but just debt free and saving, so we do have some money to splurge.

But I haven't really been much of a beach person. When I was younger, the beach actually disturbed me. With sensitive blue eyes, the bright sun reflected in the white sand and water made me squint. No fun to scrunch your face up all day. The brilliant sun attacked my fair skin with a vengeance, often causing blisters in the days before sunscreen. And my hair! The relentless wind coupled with the humidity destroyed any order in my locks, an embarrassment for my young appearance-conscious self.

But when we moved back to Ohio and started to endure long winters again, a beach break became more attractive. Then my retired friends started going to Myrtle Beach in the winter and inviting me to join them for a week in their rented condo. I learned to wear sunglasses, don sunscreen and couldn't care less about my hair. Ah, the freedom of growing wiser with the ability to focus on the more important things in life!

In January, once again I visited my friends at a condo at Surfside Beach, South Carolina. Fortunate to be escaping Ohio cold, I relished time to relax with several friends and savor the beach. The first morning, I received yet another letter from the Earth, so full of wisdom and good advice. I am most grateful.

The Letter

Hello Nancy,

I'm so glad you decided to take a break at the beach of your life.

Here is a place to slow down and savor each day. Welcome the sunrise. Let go at sunset. Experience the dazzling beauty where water waves into land.

For eons, you humans come here to dwell in the beauty to get away from your ordinary life. In warmer months, you swim and sun, in colder months, you walk.

Open yourself to this place. Open your heart to spaciousness. Let that mighty shore teach you what it is you need at this point in your life.

I am always here, welcoming you while we live together. Absorb the beauty so you will hold it within when you return to your inland life.

Love,
Your Gaia God.

My Response

This letter felt like a message, "Welcome to my World, Nancy! Enjoy!" I took the Earth's instructions to heart as I began my week at the beach. I hurried out in the mornings with my camera to drink in the sunrises. In the evenings, I took time to look up and observe the colors as day shifted into night. I spent time just absorbing the spaciousness of the beach.

I also took the message to relax seriously, focusing on enjoying vacation. Some days, I didn't go out for sunrise. One day, I just lay down in the sun inside the condo, and even there I felt the spaciousness and the warmth of the beach.

And now, I hold that beauty inside of me, with many photos to share when I returned home with a deeper sense of connection to the beach.

A Letter from the Earth about Love at the Beach-January 19, 2016

Introduction

When visiting my friends at the beach, I wanted a traveling companion. One of my favorite friends, Heidi Berkenbosch, from Prairie City, Iowa, agreed to go with me. She drove from Iowa to Ohio in the cold of winter to accompany me. Heidi loves to laugh, and she loves the beach. One day, when we walked on the beach, I asked her what it was that she most appreciates about the beach. She told me that she just likes to feel at one with the beach as she walks along. I contemplated that thought when we walked, when I went out to photograph the sunrise, when I went out to catch the sunset. What does that mean, I wondered? And how would that be different than my crazy efforts to capture the surf in its beauty through my camera lens? Should I leave my camera at home, I wondered?

I ventured from Ohio to Myrtle Beach as another part of the birthday gift of monthly experiences for my friend, Chris, who has ovarian cancer. The cancer came back this year and this time, it's inoperable. I laughed about this trip, telling her, "I gave you a birthday present, inviting myself to spend a week with you at the beach!" She laughed, too. We didn't know if they could even make the trip, so the present was a gift of hope back in July. I hoped her cancer would stay in check, or better yet just go away. But ovarian cancer seems particularly good at resurgence.

Spending time with Chris and her husband, Dave, at Myrtle Beach during their month of condo days conjures many happy memories for us. Over the years, I've ventured down to join them several times for a few days for a winter break. We remember card games, a crazy Mardi Gras parade and night at Dick's Last Resort, dining and explorations, time at Brookgreen Gardens and time on the beach at Huntington Beach State Park. During the off season of winter, the days are cooler and sometimes downright cold. But if you get a good sunny day, you can enjoy the warmth of the beach with a blanket and coat. We love to remember the day several years ago when we spent the afternoon sitting on the beach with our other friend Karol. Dave brought pretzels and proceeded to feed the gulls. I took picture after picture of him, the Pied Piper of Sea Gulls, I called him and later made the photos into a little book for them with a poem of gratitude, recreating that wonderful sunny afternoon at Huntington Beach State Park.

If you ever go to Myrtle Beach, take some time to venture south to Brookgreen Gardens and the state park. Brookgreen Gardens includes an outdoor sculpture garden and interpretative park, exposing the evils of slavery which once visited this location. In the 1930s, Anna Hyatt, a sculptress, married Archer Huntington, a wealthy poet. When she developed a lung disease, the doctor told her to spend her winter out of New York City where they lived. So, they purchased four old plantations in South Carolina and proceeded to build "Atalaya', their beach home, in the style of a Scottish Moor Castle. The house included outdoor rooms where Anna could observe and sculpt horses, monkeys and other animals. Later, they developed the sculpture garden to display her work, along with work of many other artists. When I visit, I always marvel at their ingenuity and am inspired by their decision to start this project when they were both over 50 years old.

During this trip, Chris didn't feel very good. Heidi and I explored Brookgreen alone. But on a sunny day, Chris and Dave agreed to join us for a journey to Huntington Beach State Park. We started by touring Atalaya. I purchased the walking tour headphones for Heidi, so she could get a good orientation to the large home. Chris and I, who visited in the past, just walked through, reading the signs and chatting. We sat down on a bench in the courtyard after we walked, waiting for Heidi, talking.

Chris didn't talk much about her cancer. She would tell us that she felt sick most of the time now, and she really couldn't start her day's activities until around 11 a.m. and then would go to bed early as well. The elephant in the room seemed to be that the cancer kept growing, and this particular round of chemo caused many side effects and didn't seem to be shrinking the cancer as much as the previous treatments did.

I felt a sense of foreboding about the whole thing. I did not want to lose my friend. I met Chris in my early days in Springfield. We shared a background in the Mennonite church, both "non-ethnic" Mennonites, as we were known. The Mennonites are a culture unto themselves, but a quite diverse lot at that. Some of us outsiders are attracted to the "primary, alternative community" of their way of doing church, as well as to their focus on deep faith, simple lifestyle and nonviolence.

While Chris' husband finished his years at Navistar, a factory in town, Chris volunteered two days a week with me at the City in my work of listening to citizens related to landlord-tenant, fair housing and neighbor conflicts. She impressed me with her generosity of time and spirit, being with me in the job of caring for the people who called. I felt a deep sense of gratitude to her for this gift of accompaniment. Many of the people I talk with each day struggle for survival on limited income, dealing with difficult housing situations. Many people say they don't know how I do my job, knowing how much complaining I hear.

But I do it as an act of service, a form of ministry, really, which keeps me going and caring. Chris understood this and approached the work in the same way. This time forged a deep bond between Chris and me. We began playing cards with our husbands and often celebrating holidays together as well. Eventually, Chris went back to work when her husband retired, before they both retired. The most frugal people I know, they specialize in living economically and figured out how to retire early to travel and enjoy life, until Chris' cancer came.

When she first learned of her cancer, shortly before her 60th birthday, a bowel obstruction led to emergency surgery at Cleveland clinic. We didn't think she had long to live. She asked me to plan a healing service for her. I mobilized some friends and soon we were developing ways to support her and Dave on this difficult journey. She defied the odds. Our prayers seemed to be heard. Now, five years later, she continued to live a miracle, but the cancer seemed to be winning.

Each person who deals with a life-threatening illness handles it differently. I don't know what my approach will be, if that time comes. Some people give up easily, say their goodbyes and leave, like my Mom. Some tenaciously hang on to life and refuse to let go. Our choices often determine the outcome, although many still die against their wills. I remember my friend, Renee, who lost a battle with lung cancer. She asked us repeatedly, "Doesn't God understand I want to live?"

Chris tends toward the latter. As we sat there, chatting, I asked her about how she felt that day and how she was thinking about her cancer, she told me, "I'm not okay with dying. I'm just not."

"That's really hard," I agreed. Letting go of life? No, Chris did not want to do that. She still had a lot of living planned for retirement with Dave. I got it. I felt very sad. "I don't want that either," I said. "I don't want to lose my friend."

When Heidi finished the tour, Dave came back from a walk and we all walked together over to the beach. Chris and Dave didn't walk far. Walking was becoming more difficult for Chris. They told us to go on.

I brought along a blanket, a hat and a book. Heidi and I walked down the beach. I stopped and put my blanket down. I watched Heidi walking, while I could also look back and see

Chris and Dave feeding the gulls, and standing together, watching the waves. I sensed their pain, the unknown, the waiting. The afternoon did not have quite the joy of the previous time we spent there a few years back, before the cancer.

I decided to dwell in the moment and focus on Heidi's approach of becoming one with the beach. I absorbed the sun. Took off my shoes and waded in the cold waters, then went back to my blanket and just sat, mesmerized by the waves and the water and the majesty of a beach afternoon. The next morning, the Earth wrote me this letter.

The Letter

Dear Nancy,

Yesterday on the beach, I surrounded you with love. Did you feel the warmth of my sun? The breath of salt air? The softness of the sand on your feet? Did you simply sink down onto your beach blanket, letting your body unwind and stop?

There in that sacred moment, you felt my presence breathing through you, warming, enlivening, caressing and sharing my beauty, nurturing your soul. These are the moments which breathe life into your veins. These are the moments we are one.

Do you understand why I call you to slow down and experience the beach? Do you get it, Nancy? I think you do. I think you feel that mystery wrapping you with delight.

So, Nancy, as your beach week continues, I call you to continue to awaken to the moments of unity when time seems suspended.

My shores stretch for miles around this earth, water gently lapping, caressing, pounding into land, making a perfect place for contemplative hope. Pay attention. Listen. Wake up. Hear my voice rippling through it all.

I love you. I want you to absorb the mystery and come home to love where all creation, all of us dwell as one. Enjoy!

Love, Gaia

My Response

Okay, so this letter underscored my friend's approach to feeling at one with the beach! I did experience the unity that day, and then the Earth helped me understand the concept even more, with this letter.

Since I began meditating and becoming a contemplative, I often hear a message to be present in this moment. But often, I find myself slipping into the past or projecting myself into the future. With Chris' cancer front and center, it's too easy to worry about the future. Once again, the Earth tells me to just be present and soak up the love. This message, coupled with the memory of the beach afternoon, becomes vivid and memorable.

I felt the warmth of the sun, bathing me in light. My eyes connected with the dunes. My soul spread itself out over the waves. I took off my shoes and let my feet dip into the chilly winter waters. I closed my eyes and meditated on the goodness of the place and I really did absorb the mystery, connecting with the Earth – with God – and felt the Oneness of the Sacred in the beauty of the moment.

So now when I think about being present, I can close my eyes and remember the beach afternoon, and then I can open my eyes and look around me and realize that the ripples of love extend even into this present moment, this current landscape and experience where I dwell. Thank you, Gaia!

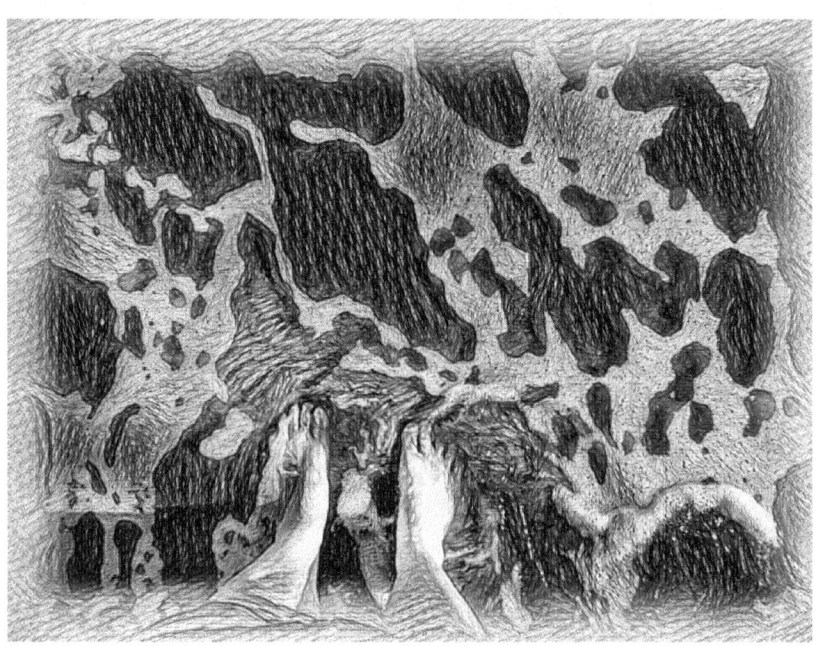

A Letter from the Earth about Sorrow at the Beach-January 20, 2016

Introduction

Have you noticed the suds on the beach? Have you heard that jellyfish are growing in population? Have you seen tar and plastics washing up on the beach? Did you know that our oceans are heating up because of climate change and that 40% of the coral is already dead? Did you hear about the 100,000 penguins that died?

When I go to the beach now, it's very hard for me to avoid thinking about the changing ocean. And yet in the past, and even on this trip, I snap picture after picture, trying very hard to keep the suds out. I don't want that ugliness reminding me that we may be polluting our oceans beyond repair. I don't want to think about what I've learned about how our pollution and the warming water is causing serious harm to the varieties of life under the sea.

The afternoon at Huntington Beach State Park when I put my feet in the ocean, I wanted to photograph the moment. But when I looked through the camera to the picture, I noticed the suds covered my feet. I didn't want them in the picture. Should I skip taking the picture, I wondered. But no, I decided to go ahead. I took a picture of my feet in the pollution. I am usually focusing on capturing the beauty of nature in my photos, so, photographing my feet in the suds was a huge step for me.

A couple days later, the Earth wrote me this letter.

The Letter

Dear Nancy,

This week at the beach, I've been watching you take in my joy mixed with sorrow. I notice it's hard for you to walk on the beach without feeling sad when you see the foam washing up on the shore. Yes, the pollution in my oceans is overbearing these days. Yesterday, you saw the jellyfish who flourish in unhealthy waters. This disturbs me as well.

Your planet took billions of years to evolve into the majesty of today and now the practices of humans are destroying so much of the tender ecosystems which made your life possible. This is big and you know it. So how then do you live?

I saw you take a picture of the foam yesterday. You photographed your feet in it the day before. And the jellyfish made it into some of your picture frames, too.

It's okay to be sad, to grieve, to express your exasperation and anguish. This is part of my message to you. Wake up. Wake them up.

Remember there are ways to restore the natural environment, but they must wake up before it's too late for your species.

So, keep walking. Keep talking. Keep photographing the good and the bad. You're on an important path of love.

Love, Gaia

My Response

When the Earth wrote me this letter, I began to realize my photography must change. I wouldn't say I've agreed to embark on this path yet, but I understand. I will eventually learn to photograph the results of our mistreatment of the earth, along with its beauty.

And here, the earth tells me to grieve. When I refused to photograph the suds, I realized I'm just as caught up in denial as my high school friends. Just like when someone dies suddenly, you want to believe it's not true. The first stage of grief, Elisabeth Kubler-Ross told us.

Perhaps I should look for the pictures that express the degradation of the Earth and practice meditating on them. Doesn't it seem like this is what the Earth is calling me to do? Maybe these pictures will be a part of my speaking up, the path of love, as she calls it.

When our loved ones are hurting, we express sympathy. We listen to their pain, we observe and acknowledge what bothers them, don't we? In this way, we express our love. So, maybe listening to the pain that our Earth is experiencing, photographing it, observing and acknowledging it will be a way I can love the Earth back, calling others to awaken and change, also.

Once again, the Earth teaches and astounds me with her wisdom and guidance. And I find myself thinking once more, "I never thought of it that way before!"

A Letter from the Earth about Avoiding Blizzard Travel-January 22, 2016

Introduction

As our week at Myrtle Beach drew to a close, I began to monitor the weather for the trip home. I knew January driving from Ohio to South Carolina and back could create problems. On the way down, we planned to visit friends and family near Asheville, in western North Carolina. But with snow predicted in the mountains, we drove directly down to South Carolina and avoided treacherous roads. Now, on the trip home, I planned to visit some of my favorite people in eastern North Carolina, Rev. Bill Salyers and his wife, Mary Jane. They retired to Springfield, Ohio, years back and became our good church friends. Mary Jane, a retired school teacher, tutored our son Jacob and helped him improve his writing for the SAT. Bill led many progressive political efforts. Mary Jane started a writers' group and nurtured me as a new writer, while she spun her own tale, using her childhood in Appalachia as a springboard for a story about a young girl growing up and coming of age in an earlier time. They moved to the Chapel Hill area to be close to their daughter, Joy, and her husband and young children. We planned to visit them on Friday, spend the night and return home on Saturday. I looked forward to introducing Heidi to my friends.

We scheduled a Thursday morning trip to visit Sandy Island, a Gullah community off the coast of South Carolina. I became interested in the Gullah people after visiting an art exhibit and program about them at Brookgreen Gardens earlier in the week. The Gullah people originally came from western Africa and developed a distinctive culture and language within the slave communities of the south. Now, many still live on islands off the coast of the southeastern United States. I wanted to learn more. When I walked the labyrinth at Brookgreen

Garden, I received a message that I should include the Gullahs in my next book. That took me by surprise, startled me actually. But I often hear God while walking a labyrinth, so I took this instruction very seriously.

However, the weather report indicated a major winter storm would be developing and would cover much of our travel area by Friday. I kept hoping that the forecast would change, but it did not. By late Wednesday, I canceled our visit with the Salyers and the Sandy Island tour as well. We left Thursday morning and hightailed it for Ohio, meeting up with my husband in Athens, Ohio at the Ohio University Inn where he was attending a conference with fellow local recycling staff from around the state. Heidi and I enjoyed free, comfortable lodging with him and only suffered a little bit of snow the next morning, before driving back home to Springfield.

We then enjoyed the luxury of a free day in Springfield, rather than spending hours on a snow-covered road. As much as I regretted the canceled visit with the Salyers and not getting to learn more about the Gullah people, I also felt so much gratitude for the weather report that saved us from driving through a winter snowstorm. On that next morning, I received this letter from the Earth.

The Letter

Dear Nancy,
This week, you had a great time at the beach and you were wise when you watched the weather forecasts and avoided a very difficult trip home.

In this modern age, you have many technologies making life easier. Use them. Take advantage of winter storm warnings. Adjust, rearrange your plans as you have done this week.

You are the fortunate ones. Live in your fortunate ways and experience life fully.

You have shelter, heat, moving vehicles, electricity, flowing water and so many modern conveniences. I am very proud of the ingenuity of modern humans.

But with the intelligence comes great responsibility. Sustainability is the catchword these days. And so I ask you to continue to speak. As the great awakening happens, you can engineer many ways through. But remind them that the natural world can reach a breaking point.

You are not alone. Millions are waking now. Be the one hundredth monkey. Speak up. Be truth in our time.

I love you, Nancy.

Your ever-evolving, Gaia God.

My Response

I was so happy to avoid the blizzard and felt doubly blessed when the Earth celebrated with me. A few weeks later, a friend canceled our lunch plans because she had to babysit her grandchildren. The other grandmother had been stranded on a tour bus on the Pennsylvania Turnpike for 3 days in that blizzard and was very sick.

The Earth is right. We are smart and fortunate. I wondered why the leaders of the other grandmother's group ignored the forecast. They certainly could check the weather report, as I did. They could have avoided being stranded for three days on the turnpike!

We can profit greatly from our scientific knowledge when we so choose. We do have so many modern conveniences. I often think that many of us living in North America in this era are some of the most blessed people in the history of our species. I grew up with adequate food, shelter and community. I attended good schools, chose my own life path, went on to college and although I faced lean times in early adulthood, never really worried much about getting my basic needs met. Now in my empty nest times, I'm able to explore my interests of photography, gardening, travel, writing and music, while continuing a meaningful job. Technologically speaking, we are quite wealthy.

But then the Earth mentions "sustainability" and reminds me of my call to speak up. I know that our path of overuse and abuse of the world's resource is catching up with us very quickly. We are on a collision path with our environment unless we begin to choose to make sustainability a choice.

Over the past several years, while becoming aware of these concerns and of my own call to speak, I do what I can. I do little things, like speaking up when the weather gets crazy. I support my husband in his leadership of our local Citizens' Climate Lobby group. I started a website for Ohioans to write a monthly letter on climate change. I keep thinking about a communication plan to get more people to take action. I am diligently working on this book and a fiction book as well with an Earth theme. Once again, the Earth offers me hope and encouragement.

Do you know the hundredth monkey phenomenon? Between 1952 and 1958, Japanese researchers studied the Macaca Fuscata monkeys. Some of the monkeys learned to wash sweet potatoes they found in the sand on the beach. They passed this on to their young monkeys and then later, the researchers discovered that monkeys on other islands were doing this as well. They hypothesized that when habit and practices become widespread, the consciousness can be transferred to others. The "hundredth monkey" concept means that the monkeys reached the critical threshold to cause this shift of consciousness among all the monkeys.

If it happened with the monkeys, could consciousness shifts cause change in human behavior as well? Although at times, it seems that we are very slow as a people to acknowledge and act on environmental degradation, the voices have been growing for many years now. The book *Blessed Unrest* compiles information on grass-root organizations. Over a million groups are organizing for change. Here, the Earth empowers me with this letter to speak up and join the others. Together, I pray that we will bring the shift to a new way of sustainable living. I pray that I am indeed the "hundredth monkey."

Letters from the Earth

Received by Nancy Flinchbaugh

A Letter from the Earth Encouraging Me to Continue Listening-January 25, 2016

Introduction

    Over half a year passed, and I continued to receive the letters from the Earth. I posted quite a few on my webpage, and usually posted a link on Facebook, without much response. Facebook likes tend to go for the sensational and quirky. When I ride my bike to work, I get quite a few likes. Over a hundred one day when I posted a picture of me with my bike in front of my office cubicle. I also received a hundred when I completed my first triathlon. Sometimes I get 50 likes for just posting one of my nature photos.

    Although I didn't receive a lot of comments or likes about my letters from the Earth, occasionally friends would mention they were reading them and they liked them. Whenever I shared them directly with someone, I would get affirmation. And, I began to realize that the letters were a wonderful present for me personally. I hoped eventually others might love them, too, but I knew even if I were the only one to ever hear and appreciate them, they were truly splendid epistles, having a wonderful rippling effect in my life.

I came home after the trip to the beach and started to get back in my routine. I felt rested and enthused, ready to go back to work. I appreciated the Earth's comments at the beach and on the trip home. I noticed I heard more when I slowed down on vacation, which didn't surprise me. Still in a slower mode the morning I prepared to return to work, I received this letter.

The Letter

Dear Nancy,

Thank you for listening to me. Your discipline is bearing fruit.

You are learning to celebrate and appreciate the life we share. You are learning to marvel at the miracles unfolding constantly around you. You are learning to savor your food.

At the same time, you are learning to speak up, to call others to awaken and not to give up in speaking for me, for the natural world that we share.

I applaud your willingness to receive these letters from me. I will keep writing as long as you are listening.

Enjoy the adventure of your day and yes, check out the possibilities of dance lessons. You won't be disappointed. Thank you for taking seriously my instructions to dance!

Love, Gaia

My Response

When I received this letter, I began to realize how much the Earth taught me in such a short period of time. Such good advice!

It's a weird thing to receive these letters. I keep asking

myself, "Is it really me writing?" Obviously, I am writing, and yet the insights come from beyond me. I often find myself thinking, "Oh! I never thought of it quite like that before."

And then I wonder if someday, the letters will quit coming. If they were to go viral, would the letters stop?

So here, where the Earth tells me she will keep writing as long as I am listening, I feel very happy. I have come to trust her, and so I believe her when she tells me this.

Now about the dance lessons. I had to mull that over for a while. My husband and I have taken some over the years... Swing, contra, square, two-step and most recently, waltz. We sort of get it, but we're not going to win any dance contests, if you know what I mean?

But should I take lessons by myself?

I must admit I have an inferiority complex when it comes to dance. Maybe that is widespread. Maybe that is why so many people absolutely refuse to dance. It rarely stops me! But I've had just enough negative feedback about my dancing to think maybe it should!

I remember having a deliriously wonderful time a few years back, dancing at a fundraiser for an African-American women's service club. They had a couple lines going which would cause you to dance alone while everyone cheered your moves on. They made appropriate noises and affirmations for my prancing and gyrating, but when I returned to my seat, my companion told me I didn't have rhythm!

A couple months back, I was at a trivia night with some friends and felt the urge to get up and dance. I told my companions and one of them told me not to do it. No one else was dancing, but the music called me. Just a night in a bar, without a dance floor or a band, but a little gyrating would have awakened my inner muse and probably drawn some smiles from the others gathered.

Why did she tell me not to dance? Why shouldn't I dance? Later, she told me she didn't want me to embarrass myself. Because no one else was dancing and because I had a beer and felt happy, she was concerned I'd make a fool of myself.

The bigger question here for me was why I didn't dance.

I wanted to dance because I was high on life and I wanted to express my joy. I allowed her firm "NO" to stop and upset me. And I regretted it then and later.

All our lives, there are people who tell us not to dance in so many ways. And then there's the voice of my friend, Gaia, here who calls me to dance again and again and that's the voice I want to honor. That's the voice I want to hear. That's the voice of God calling me to celebrate this one short life I've been given.

One of my favorite church experiences has been designing dances with other friends and doing them in worship. I remember one Easter in San Antonio, we danced with scarves to Sandi Patty's song "Was it a morning like this?" I still remember making those scarves go in the arc of the sun.... "He is risen, He is risen, alleluia!" I remember sitting down and feeling so very alive and ready to celebrate Easter. And I also remember some people complaining about the dancing, both there and in the church where I am now. I get the impression they have a problem with imperfect bodies giving glory to God with imperfect dances, or maybe they just don't want unusual things in worship.

So, the idea of taking lessons in dance at my advanced age of 60 gave me pause. Could I do that? Would it be okay for my plump self to show up at the dance studio to learn? I found myself yearning to learn ballet.

I continue to puzzle over so many people's resistance to dance, both for themselves and sometimes for me. I feel sad that so many don't participate in this exuberant aspect of being alive. And I so appreciate the Earth's call to dance, to take lessons and keep on kicking up my feet! Touche!

A Letter from the Earth concerning the Animals-January 26, 2016

Introduction

    Through my life, I have usually been blessed with an animal or two living with me. In my childhood home, my parents wanted us to grow up with some four-legged companions. The first cat I remember, Candy, gave birth to four kittens. We watched the miracle of birth and participated in naming the little ones. Her babies became "Lollipop" (the calico), Taffy and Carmel (the buff-colored ones) and Gumdrop (the grey one). And I remember that Candy went crazy after becoming a mother and we couldn't keep her very long after that. We gave all the kittens away, and eventually her as well.

    Next, we had Peppy, who was spayed, so we wouldn't have another crazy cat. She lived with us through most of the rest of my growing-up years. I loved playing and sleeping with her. My brothers and I fought over sleeping rights. My mother made peace by writing our names on the kitchen calendar. "Bruce", "Nancy" or "Paul" would appear on each calendar square so we could consult the calendar at night and not fight about the cat.

Now in my work as a fair housing coordinator, the disability part of the law requires landlords to allow people to have companion animals to help with mental health issues. This makes the landlords mad, because it's not very difficult to get a health care professional to write a note that someone needs a pet. But, you probably know that having a pet in the home is therapeutic for all of us. Research tells us that people with pets live longer, have lower blood pressure and tend to be happier.

My husband and I have lost two animals in recent years. First, our dog Layla, and then our cat Sugar. Our home felt very empty. However, we didn't think we could handle an animal again until we retired, because the animal would be alone most of the time. But one day, my coworker, Ed, made a comment about how he had a cat for us. He and his wife nurture the neighborhood cats and go so far as to take them to the vet and get them spayed. I laughed at the thought. "My husband is allergic to cats!" I told him.

But later, when I told Steve about the cat, he told me to bring her home and we could try it. (He's not allergic to all cats). So last October, my coworker and his wife brought this stray cat, Rosie, over with some food and she quickly adapted to our household. I felt good about adopting a homeless cat, and we both enjoyed having an animal in the house with us again. We named her Emily Rose, because we picked out the name "Emily" for the daughter we never had.

I noticed with our previous cat, Sugar, that her purring seems to be a form a meditation. So I always welcomed her to sit with me during meditation, and soon Emily joined me as well. Sometimes she sits with me on my lap and then after a while, goes to sit on another chair and just seems to hang out with me in the morning that way. One day, as she sat there with me, I thought about how much I appreciate her presence, and the Earth wrote me this letter.

The Letter

Dear Nancy,

In your house, you have a new family member, Emily Rose. Now she sits with you on your easy chair, as together you contemplate morning. Since she found you over a year ago now, I've watch you bond. She seeks you out for lap-sitting. You seek her out for a chilling-out buddy. You keep each other warm in the winter.

She's with you and also apart. She jumps up abruptly to go do her thing. She bats at you with her paw if you move unexpectedly. She has a mind of her own.

Have you noticed how some people are so in tune with animals? Remember your husband with your dog, Layla? Think about those people called to be veterinarians, to work with animals.

There is a mystery there and also a wildness. Remember the woman, Amy, at church who spoke about the connections she has with the horses and animals in her farm? Remember the stories about the previous owner of your house who fed the birds who migrated back to this place every year and who cared for injured animals in the room upstairs?

You applaud efforts of people like the Leinasars who pay attention to cats in their neighborhood. Because of their great sensitivity, you acquired Sugar, a companion cat for your mother in later years and then for you and Steve after your mom passed on. And now, they brought you Emily Rose.

I am calling you to be more attentive to the animals. Listen. Watch. Care. You will learn from them more about me.

Love, Gaia

My Response

Usually when I get a letter from the Earth, the directions resonate with who I am and who I am striving to be. But this one was a little like the original letter. She wants me to start a blog? No, I don't have time for that! And now she wants me to start caring for the animals? No, Gaia, I don't have time for that either!

I really appreciate the people who do this, but that is their calling, not mine, I think. Certainly I care for my cat, and have taken care of other pets well through the years, but after that, I draw a line.

And yet I realize that our last three pets, two cats and a dog, were rescued by these people who pay attention. Our beloved Layla was rescued by our friends, Linda and Margaret, who saw her dumped in the park across from their house. What if they hadn't paid attention? Ed and Shelley found Sugar and Emily roaming in their neighborhood, took them to the vet and eventually turned them over to us. What if they hadn't paid attention?

As I consider my knee-jerk negative response, I know I will be coming around on this eventually. I hear my response is similar to the perspective that says the humans are the important ones and we don't need to worry too much about the rest of creation. I know this is misguided even as I resist. This sort of thinking got us into the mess we are in today. I know we are a part of creation and that we need to honor each aspect of creation. I also know that the fact that I believe I am too busy to care for the animals is a sign that my priorities need to change.

I'm going to sit with this suggestion for a while and see where it takes me. And for now, I let my cat in and out, feed her, pet her and welcome her onto my lap, knowing we need each other. I suspect I need the other animals as well.

A Letter from the Earth Concerning a Walk in the Arboretum-January 31, 2016

Introduction

    We are fortunate to live a half block away from a beautiful cemetery and arboretum. I love to experience the seasons there, walking among tombstones from several centuries, observing trees of incredible variety. There, I often feel transported into a different place and time. On this particular day, when I walked in the arboretum, I was trying to be more mindful, but needed to use my imagination. In the middle of a warm winter, no snow covered the ground. Bare trees towered over the brown, green and muddy slopes. The somewhat tired landscape seemed mundane.

    I left my house in an older neighborhood, built in the

1920s. For sale signs stand on duplexes nearby. The sun is shining, but the view seemed rather bleak. If I focus on the economic situation here, which I know too well, working as I do in community development at our city, I could be depressed. The houses are well kept, however, as I walk down the sidewalk past the cemetery monument store and cross the street into Ferncliff Cemetery and Arboretum.

Now I relax a bit, surrounded by the trees and take a few pictures. My camera accompanies me often on walks and through its lens, I see the mundane with new eyes. On this day, I focused on the branches, so beautiful in their variety, etching portraits against the sky. And then I decided to think about my place here in the vast universe.

In my recent learning journey, I have learned New Creation stories that place us in a vast universe almost beyond comprehension. Conceived of a supernova, our planet became debris circling our sun and through an incredibly miraculous process, water brought the possibility of life. 4.7 billion years later, here we are, conscious beings, miracles in motion on this tiny planet in the colossal Milky Way, a part of an infinite Universe. I rarely think about this, but on this day, I really had a sense of me, suspended in space, on our little Earth, a part of this incredible mystery.

Conceptually, I know I'm standing on the earth. From out there in space, I might be visible as a tiny speck, if at all, here on the North American continent, on the eastern edge of the Midwest, here in Springfield, Ohio.

Often, as I walk through the cemetery, I read the names and think about the people who lived here in days gone by. On this day, I considered instead the slight curvature of the earth, probably more due to the natural hills and landscaping. But I did really sense the earth, suspended in space in orbit around the sun. I did imagine the sun star in the Milky Way and I tried to fathom that there are literally billions of such stars out there. And as I walked, I considered the story of our planet, evolving over eons to this state of incredible diversity, my home.

Later that day, I went over to Beavercreek to meet with some high school friends for lunch. Since I have begun to awaken, I want others to as well. Last year, when I met with them for our annual gift exchange and luncheon, I gave them books about climate change. They never talked to me about the books.

I asked one of them several times if my husband and I could meet with her and her husband for dinner to discuss this. I gathered from what she said that her husband, a successful stockbroker, was a climate change denier. I also know how important it is to build political support on this issue. We are gaining ground and I am ever hopeful, but she never even responded.

So this year, I brought them more traditional gifts. The early January day we met for lunch was unseasonably warm. As I greeted them in the foyer of the Olive Garden, one commented on how warm it was. I just said offhandedly, "Global warming, well, yeah."

She said, "Oh, don't start that," with a tone in her voice suggesting disgust.

I bristled. I shut up. I tucked the thought away, but tears rolled down my soul, deep inside.

The next day Gaia wrote me this letter.

The Letter

Dear Nancy,

Thank you for listening to me. So many are disconnected from me these days. I appreciate your willingness to listen and record my thoughts. Thank you very much. These walks are good for you and good for me.

For once, you took time to really consider your place in the universe. An earthling walking on planet Earth, you sensed the position of your body on a round ball, suspended in space, in an ever-evolving universe. Looking at the limestone cliffs, grown of over millions of years of geological events, now full of holes, eroding, yet still standing, you saw yourself within the Universe Story and marveled at the miracle of it all.

Thank you for taking time to be aware of all that has transpired and all that is happening now.

I know it was hard for you yesterday when your high school friends laughed and told you global warming wasn't real. Later, your husband reminded you that denial is a very real part of grief. You have to love the people, even as you continue to speak. Remember the hospice nurse, Patty Babian, who told you never to deny people their denial. Sometimes that's the best place to be.

So much churning within you these days, Nancy. I know it's painful and beautiful. Puzzling and triumphant. Depressing and hopeful.

In the midst of this time, I thank you for listening. I give thanks as you lead the church children in their dance of gratitude this morning, know that I am there, animating you and them, dancing, providing life for all and I appreciate you.

Love, Gaia

My Response

I love the line from Thornton Wilder's play, "Our Town," where the young girl, Emily, dies, and then returns to observe her family and friends carrying on with their lives. From the other side, the miracle of each moment is so clear to her, but the people she can watch, but not actually communicate with anymore, don't see this. And so she asks, "Does any human being really realize life as they live it --every, every minute?"

Emily is right. We hardly ever realize this life, and how incredible each moment can be. My new understandings of the universe often remain theoretical, but on this day they became part of my reality, as I for a moment, I truly realized the dazzling miracle of my life, suspended in a vast universe, as I walked in Ferncliff.

When the earth thanked me for doing this, I smiled. I don't think many think of this very much at all. But let me tell you, it is mind blowing! Try it sometime.

I also appreciated that Gaia talked to me about my high school friends.

Let them have their denial, the Earth tells me. Love them.

A Letter from the Earth Concerning Death-February 2, 2016

Introduction

On Sundays, my husband and I like to visit the YMCA after church. I love swimming. On this particular Sunday, I swam my half mile and then we came home, preparing to enjoy an afternoon and evening of leisure. I made some lunch and sat down at the dining room table when I received a phone call from my younger brother, Paul.

"Have you heard about Bruce?" he asked. Bruce was our older brother. "They've been trying to reach you."

"No," I said. "No, what happened?"

"He fell this morning," Paul said. "It doesn't look good. They've taken him to the hospital, and they are getting ready to do emergency surgery."

Suddenly, my life turned upside down, and I tried to

comprehend this message. "I'll call Mary," I said. Mary was Bruce's wife.

"Yes, you should," Paul told me.

I dialed the number and connected with my sister-in-law, Mary, at the hospital with her son John and his wife, Jessica, an internal medicine resident. "Here, I'll let Jessica explain," Mary said.

She handed the phone to Jessica, who told me that Bruce fell in his kitchen, hit his head on the hard tile floor and was transported to the ER and that now they were doing emergency surgery. Jessica said, "You should come." She went on to explain that there was extensive bleeding on the brain and they were trying to stop the bleeding, but were not sure they could save him.

Earlier in the week, I talked to Bruce about planning our summer reunion. He excitedly told me about their plan to fly to California on February 4 to be in the studio audience to watch their daughter, Anne, as a contestant on Wheel of Fortune. Then they would take a cruise to Mexico before returning to Dallas. On Saturday, the day before, I talked to him briefly after he ran 16 miles, preparing for a marathon. And now? He might be dying?

My life suddenly seemed suspended in confusion. We started packing, called our bosses to ask for time off and in a few hours, we were on the road, driving overnight the 1,000-mile trek to Dallas, Texas, while I tried to comprehend this new reality. Was he really dying? Was there no hope?

Sometime during the long drive, Bruce showed up in my mind's eye. He was balling his fists, making a noise of pure joy as he entered into the heavenly realm, and I just happened to get to peek in on his excitement. It was an expression I knew well from our childhood. Whenever he would get excited about something, he would squeeze his hands into fists, move them back and forth while making a strange motor noise. There I saw him one last time, my brother, who spent his work life coordinating research and development for Texas Instruments, excited about technological things, now completely mesmerized with the hereafter.

For some reason, the newly departed often visit me. It reminded me of the time my Mom almost died, a month before she really did. I was on a tour in Athens, Greece, when all a sudden, I experienced bright lights of joy as she walked up some steps and reunited with those loved ones already passed over. I felt happy for her, but then sad as I wondered what it all meant. Later, I called the hospital where I learned she almost died the night before. When I arrived at the hospital a few days later, I asked her about what I saw. She said, "Yes, I was with them and I didn't want to come back." She then asked me for permission to die and left us to join them a few weeks later.

Maybe Bruce would come back, too, I thought. Or maybe he's already passed over? I wondered if my mind was just making this up. But remembering how I validated the experience I shared with my mom, I really didn't think so. My brother, who always did get fascinated with the amazing aspects of life, seemed to be totally excited about the new experience of passing over. I tucked away this glimpse of him for future reference.

Meanwhile, we continued driving and arrived at my brother's house early Monday morning. My younger brother, Paul, and his wife, Angela, who drove up from Brownsville the day before, waited for us and then drove us over to the hospital where we joined Mary with his children at his bedside. Soon, the doctors were telling us that he could not recover although he looked like he was just sleeping in the bed. Mary invited hospice in.

By evening time, we each said our goodbyes. Then they started morphine, took out the breathing tube and he slipped away quietly. We were left alone. I remember being there, in that hospital room, without him, thinking how I lost my father, then my mother, and now my older brother. From my original nuclear family, only Paul and I remained among the living.

The next day, I woke up crying in my brother's house and the Earth wrote me this letter.

The Letter

Dear Nancy,

I am grieving with you today. So much loss for you and your family to lose your brother.

I know that death is hard for you and other earthlings. All of a sudden, the person is gone, absent, a life over. It's hard to comprehend and so sad.

Death is part of each life. I don't know if you like it that way, but I couldn't find a better way to design things. I did my best. But accidents happen, disease, permutations and always death.

I do take you all up into a spiritual realm when you die, so it's not as painful as you may think. You've heard stories and had a few glimpses. All so true.

So just slow down and allow your sadness to be. I am with you and your family, even as you grieve.

Love, Gaia

My Response

When I received this letter, I felt very grateful for two reasons: 1) the Earth offered love and explanation and 2) the Earth affirmed the afterlife.

Death is hard to understand. Unexpected death IS even harder to take. We thought my marathon-running brother was the picture of health. What can anybody do to make us feel better at a time like this? What I know for sure is that only love can cushion the grieving heart. As we held each other, shared stories of my incredible brother's life and prepared his funeral, it was love that carried us through. My friends sent letters, cards, posted care on Facebook, called to listen to me, showering me with love. And so this letter from the earth was exactly what I needed at that time.

And then, the Earth apologized! Saying that was the only way she could figure out how to make life. I never thought of it that way before! I mean, how would one go about creating life? Maybe life requires death? Okay. I have to take her word on this one.

She explains that lives do transition into the spirit world and once again, I found myself smiling inside. That truth is one I know for sure and my belief just got a whole lot stronger when I received this letter.

I remembered the experience I had of Bruce entering the

spiritual realm on the way down to Dallas. I thought about my mom's experience when she almost died that one night. I thought of others who visited me shortly after their death, and I kept smiling. And it just felt good to hear the Earth explaining how she set it up for us to pass into the spirit world when we die, and to know my brother just joined them all on the other side. When I told my niece, she said she wasn't ready to hear that yet. But for me, early on, it was such a great comfort to sense my brother and then to hear this from the Earth.

A Letter from the Earth concerning Natural Healing-February 10, 2016

Introduction

One thing I've realized about life over the years is the many choices we make about how we care for our bodies. My mother advocated natural healing techniques. She worked with Dr. Hay in a Pocono Mountain retreat in the 1940s where they cured arthritis with colonics and natural diets of fruits and vegetables. She taught me to do what I could to take good care of my body.

Our modern life seems to brim with stress. In the winter, flu and cold hit hard. I try to avoid getting sick, but sometimes I forget to take care of myself. Soon, the stress of my brother's death caught up with me. I didn't plan to be gone from work that week, I found myself too busy trying to catch up and launch three events I coordinated in the two weeks after I returned. As I walked through my time of grief, I pushed myself to make up for lost time.

In the morning, when I came to meditation, I knew I didn't feel very good. I felt my body starting to get run down. I decided to listen to a relaxation meditation that I acquired while trying to help my friend Chris deal with her cancer. I thought back to the day she called, totally stressed out. I suggested that she listen to this meditation. She forgot I gave it to her, but looked through her cds and found it there. Later, she told me that when she listened to it, she relaxed for the first time in a long time and went to sleep.

I learned to appreciate this guided meditation as well, which was developed for cancer patients to relax and imagine healing flowing through the body. I often went to sleep, listening. But on this day, I stayed awake, and after the meditation, I began to journal and sensed the Earth wanted to speak. I received this letter:

The Letter

Dear Nancy,

This morning, you felt an illness coming on and you decided to listen to that healing meditation of yours. Thank you for letting your body have a break and some encouragement.

When you are going through rough times, it's important to relax. Your body can heal itself. I designed it that way, but it also requires that you let it get rest, water and good food.

Do you know why there is so much disease today? There is so much dis-ease with life and stress causes all kinds of illness. Your pollution of our environment doesn't help.

I want you to be very good to your body each day so that you can more fully enjoy your life and live your unique gifts.

So slow down. Take time to laugh. Connect with people. Love. Plan parties. Did you almost forget that today is Mardi Gras? Have some fun. Go out to eat. Laugh. Be Human.

Love, Gaia

My Response

Life can be very difficult these days. Most people I know are too busy. Stress seems normal and expected. I think I try very hard to take care of myself. I'm not always good at it. Most people I know tell me I do too much.

In the aftermath of my brother's death, I tried very hard to catch up. When I received this letter, I started to get run down. I stopped. I took care of myself with the meditation. And as I did that, I received this letter reminding me to do this and affirming this action. It resonated deeply with my spirit

Here the Earth reminds me that the human body is designed to heal itself. When we get sick, we tend to run to the doctor, but really, maybe what we should try first is to relax?

They say we get cancers all the time, but usually our immune system cures us. It's only when we are stressed that the cancer takes hold. Likewise, now that doctors try very hard to limit antibiotics, we usually have to get over colds and minor infections on our own. And as the Earth says, so many illnesses are caused by stress. I read that the majority of doctor visits are triggered by emotional upsets.

My son, Jacob, once told me, "You never get sick." I like to believe this about myself, although it's not always true. I try to teach him my strategies because he gets sick a lot more than me. I realize I've been learning slowly what the Earth tells me in this letter.

I will continue to do what I think brings me health. I exercise regularly. I try to eat well. I take time to relax each day. I meditate each morning to clear my mind and then listen for God and get a good start to my day. This process helps me live my "unique gifts," as the Earth says. And I will remember that my body will usually heal itself, if I can take good care.

And then at the end of this letter, the Earth encouraged me to celebrate Mardi Gras. I love to celebrate Mardi Gras, but it comes in the middle of the week, and the only time I really remember having a good go at it was a few years ago when I was at the beach with Chris and Dave on vacation when it came around. We attended a little parade in a shopping mall and then went to the ridiculously decadent restaurant, Dick's Last Resort, where I bought everyone a very large souvenir glass full of beer, and then had to finish them all off. Dave took a video of me swinging my Mardi Gras beads to a song and we still laugh together when we remember that night.

But here I was, early morning on Mardi Gras 2016, getting this letter telling me to celebrate. I was grieving my brother and a party was out of the question. But dinner out seemed doable and possibly a genuine pick-me-up. Never too late, the Earth seemed to say.

When my husband came downstairs, I told him the Earth wanted me to go out to eat for Mardi Gras. He said, "Well, did you tell the Earth that you are going out to eat tomorrow night?"

I laughed.

"I don't want to go out tonight, also," he explained.

"That's okay," I assured him. "You don't have to go. I'll find someone else."

And I did. My two Tiffany friends agreed to meet me at the steakhouse. One brought her husband and daughter, the other her son. I visited the dollar store during an afternoon break and found Mardi Gras table decorations, necklaces and even a valentine vase for each of us so we could be prepared for the next holiday coming soon.

That evening, we had a happy time of it, pledging to celebrate future holidays together. They did spend quite a bit of time listening to my grief, because it was our first visit since I returned from my brother's funeral. But also, we donned our beads and laughed.

These friends are my family here, since our sons left town for Seattle and Boston. And I felt so loved that they could come out to eat with me at the drop of the hat and help me follow the Earth's suggestion.

If the Earth hadn't suggested a celebration, I would have let Mardi Gras go by without some fun. Do you see how Gaia transforms my life into goodness? My gratitude overflows in return.

A Letter from the Earth on Valentine's Day-February 14, 2016

Introduction

After my brother died, we gathered in Dallas to say goodbye, trying to comprehend this great tragedy. Our sons flew in from Seattle and Boston. My cousins, whom I rarely see, came from Arizona, Tennessee, and North Carolina. My sister-in-law's brothers came with their wives from California and Minnesota. We were very sad, but the one thing that also was so good about that gathering was the love we shared and continue to share with each other.

Many showered us with love. Coworkers of my younger brother, Paul, provided a barbeque feast. Mary's daughter-in-law's parents provided Chinese food another night. My nephew John's workplace treated us to an Italian dinner. We felt well-cared for as we worked with Mary, John and Anne to prepare the funeral services. We kept alive the family tradition of playing the card game "Oh Heck" and other games during the week. We made plans to stay in touch better in the weeks and months ahead. My nephew John said, "We're going to need you to get through this, you know."

So then, on Valentine's Day, I received this Valentine from the Earth.

The Letter

Dear Nancy,

On Valentine's Day, I want you to know I love you. That is the spark of all life, you know. From the beginning, I've longed for someone to talk with, to be with, to create with. You fulfill all my imaginings when you love.

So, keep on loving. Please cherish life. So fragile, so amazing, so spectacular, until you too spiral out of this world.

Each person, each animal, all of this created world, I ask you to lavish with love. Your scripture tells you the greatest of faith, hope and love is love and it's so true.

I celebrate the love you humans share and I'm there in the midst of it, cheering you on and beating your hearts and celebrating with you the miracles love unfolds.

Yes, Nancy, love is the greatest aspect of all my creation. Be love. Share love. Fulfill all my dreams for you.

Happy Valentine's Day. I love you, Gaia God

My Response

Wow! When I got this letter, I really "loved" it! I posted it on Facebook with a picture of my family gathered at my brother's funeral, holding a picture of him, because the love we shared at that time was so real and tangible and carrying us through. And when I saw my sister-in-law, Mary, my brother's wife, "liked it" on Facebook, I knew the letter was not just for me, but for her as well.

As a Christian, I've always believed that God is love and that all things were created through love and that loving God and each other are the two greatest commandments. So, this letter shouldn't really be terribly surprising to me. And yet, it just seemed so real, so right, and so good to me in the midst of my grief.

As I've mentioned before, we still have quite a lot, like 95%, mystery in creation. That mystery? That spark? That connection? That which runs through all and in all? That's love. I really believe it.

So she's given me my marching orders. The best I can do will be to love. And I intend to do as much of this as I humanly can.

Yes, ma'am. I love you, too, Gaia. Thank you for this incredible Valentine. I will cherish it forever.

A Letter from the Earth calling for Connection-February 20, 2016

Introduction

Over the winter, we tend to spend a lot of time inside. Each cold day fades into the next. Outdoors scenery turns forlorn, browns and greys spread out across the land. In my grief, the indoor view started to seem sad and tired, as well.

There are times in all of our lives when we have more questions than answers. Sometimes people let us down. In the aftermath of my brother's death, I found it harder to laugh. On the day I received this letter, I began my day as usual, with meditation and journaling. I found myself asking questions, grappling with emotions of my own and others' anger, confusion, loneliness, absence, distrust. When I stopped to listen to God, I received yet another Letter from the Earth.

The Letter

Dear Nancy,

Keep observing the earth.

You feel like a stranger in your own home today. Sometimes I think you humans are strangers on planet Earth because you have become so disconnected from me.

Spend time outdoors and you will not be lonely. Walk to work and you will understand. Listen to the wind. Watch the flowers grow. Plant. Harvest. Observe the seasons.

Right now, we are reaching the end of winter in Ohio. The cold is leaving. Buds begin to appear. The ground thaws. Although the days are still cold, the seeds and plants are starting to awaken.

Nancy, don't get too caught up in the human drama. You are of the earth. Clay animated. Stardust, if you will. This is the stuff of life. You have all these modern trappings, but remember you emerged, just like a plant. And just like all living things, eventually, you die. Don't be too caught up in all of your head stuff.

Take time to be and seek me in nature. Connect with fallow ground. Experiment a little more with bringing your own plot of land to life this year.

And remember to dance. Now is the time. Don't wait for tomorrow.

Love,
Gaia

My Response

Have you heard about that nonprofit called, "No Child Left Inside"? This organization funds projects to get children outdoors, connecting with the Earth. Many people are beginning to sense that that we are, as a society, becoming too disconnected from the Earth, and that we need to turn this trend around.

My paternal grandparents were farmers. Only three generations ago, the majority of Americans lived on farms.

Change came so quickly during the industrial age. In 150 years, we left the farms for the cities. Perhaps our lives became easier, and perhaps they have become something God never intended. We seem to have become so disassociated from the Earth that we are able to destroy our environment without a second thought. The businesses can do what they want in search of money and the "tree huggers" are laughed down.

One thought from Brian Swimme's book *The Hidden Heart of Cosmos* stays with me. He suggests that the reason we have so much depression and drug and alcohol addiction is because we are focused on "dead things". So much of what we strive to acquire are things: the latest electronic product or gadget, the latest car. Our materialism drives us to drink, take drugs and become depressed. Why? Because we were intended to be in relationship with the Earth and people. Dead things won't fulfill our deep spiritual need for love and that connectedness with God, others and all of creation.

This letter once again resonates with what I have been learning. I knew the Earth got it right here.

I went outside and started to walk around my yard, remembering my flower beds last year and planning how I would I improve them this year. I visited the vegetable garden and started clearing it out. I called a friend who likes to start her plants inside and always shares some with me to discuss what she's growing. I began to notice the signs of spring.

And the Earth got it right. As I started to connect with the natural world, I felt more connected all around. I loved that she told me not to get too caught up in human drama. We humans can be a real trip, living in our heads and forgetting that we are clay, stardust, a part of the natural world, not separate from it. Animated clay? I loved that thought. Stardust? We're all part of heaven. Mortal? Someday, I will die.

Yes, and being part of the natural world, I will dance, like the leaves on the tree in the wind. I will dance like the blowing grasses by the beach. I will dance like the maple helicopter seeds twirling to earth to bring new life. Yes, I will dance!

A Letter from the Earth about the Dance-March 5, 2016

Introduction

As I read back over my Letters from the Earth, I find that she keeps telling me to dance. Again and again in quite a few of them. And then she told me to take dance lessons, and so I started to explore the options at the Gary Geis School of Dance, a reputable studio across the street from where I work.

I began by perusing their website. I couldn't find the class listings. Somebody told me to look on their Facebook page. Then, I took a bold move and called, leaving a message. Mark Cummings, Gary's partner, called me back and discussed the various adult classes. Although I wanted to take ballet, the jazz class fit into my schedule better. Mark encouraged me to come and observe. He said I could do the warm-ups with them.

And so, one Thursday night, I timidly headed to dance class for the first time in over 50 years. I arrived early, and watched a tap class led by Gary Geis, surprised to see several people I knew following along in the lively routines. Gary, in his 70s, seemed still in his prime as he led the adult class.

Soon the time for my class came. I took a place in the back row and started to follow Mark's instructions as we warmed up. I surprised myself by being able to keep up with the other class members. Then they started to work on a routine they began earlier. Mark would model the moves, and then we would try them out. I seemed to be able to follow along fairly well, but was happy to be in the back where I could watch others rather than be watched myself. Of course, we all showed up on the mirror in the front of the class.

At the end of the class, Mark encouraged me to come again. He told me I did very well and have a good sense of rhythm. Maybe my friend who told me I had no rhythm was wrong? I made plans to come again.

So, you see, I listen to the Earth when she tells me to dance. I won't say I've been dancing nonstop, but I definitely am looking for opportunities to dance more, and I realize this has been important to me all my life. I think the Earth sensed this when she wrote me this letter.

The Letter

Dear Nancy,

You've been taking my call to you to dance very seriously. For that, I thank you and I think you thank me, too.

You have always loved to dance and play in your life. I've watched you since you were a little girl dancing as a little Eskimo, and then a Scottish stepper. Remember baton lessons? Being a Bellette with your kicklines on the football field and the dance routines on the basketball court? Although you slowed down some, remember winning that dance contest at Lake of the Ozarks when you were in college? And even now, you and that husband of yours continue to seek opportunities to dance.

When you dance, you come alive in a very special way.

Your body moves creatively with music and rhythm. You express yourself and become a moving picture of beauty. Have you noticed how it makes you so happy inside?

You want to be fit and to exercise. Don't you see that dancing is a fun way to do that? Don't you absolutely love Water Zumba? I saw you laughing the entire hour at the YMCA pool last Saturday! Didn't you feel good after Contra dancing with Steve last Sunday? Did you just feel happy after going to the Gary Geis School of Dance fundraiser last night? You danced with the parents, the children, the teachers, the young and old, all dancing the night away without alcohol. Graceful, jazz, ballet, fun.

I'm so glad you took your first jazz class. Go back. Keep learning. Keep moving. Allow yourself to be animated from within. You will never regret the time of your life you spend in the dance.

And will you please save the next dance for me? Know I am ever present within your dance.

Love, Gaia

My Response

As I write this response to the Earth's letter, my right hand types awkwardly encased in a brace. On St. Patrick's Day, I hurried back to my office from a meeting. Walking across the City Hall plaza, a cement square slightly raised proved enough to trip me up, launching me down with my right hand and cheek slamming into the pavement. Before this, the Earth told me to slow down. If only I listened! Nevertheless, I proceeded to go to a lunch hour Scrabble tournament an hour later with my hand wrapped in a green T-shirt and win, before proceeding to the emergency room, where the male nurse told me I broke my fifth metacarpal, a "boxer" break, the type of injury boxers get. Looks like I may need to take a 6-8 week break from dancing!

And, last week, Gary Geis died. After a dance career of over 40 years, the man who taught so many Springfield residents to dance will be laid to rest on Wednesday. I want to go to his funeral. I hope someone will dance. Gary and I won't be dancing that day. Life is short, there come days we can't dance, which makes dancing when possible ever so more important.

So, now, as I work on doing what I can to assist the healing process of my hand, I have time to contemplate my future dance plans. As I read over this letter from the Earth, I realize that dancing has indeed been an important part of my life. I don't plan on stopping now.

So, Gaia, yes. I will continue to dance and I'll plan to save a magnificent first dance just for you, the day my doctor pronounces my hand healed.

A Letter from the Earth Concerning Learning with Mary Anna-March 8, 2016

Introduction

In the original Letter from the Earth last May, the Earth told me to spend time learning with my friend Mary Anna, an Earth teacher. I love Mary Anna, and even though I seek her out from time to time, she works a lot teaching and selling her tatting over the weekends and also struggles with some treatments recently that made her sick. Between my schedule and hers, it took me quite a while to fulfill this instruction from the Earth.

But, finally, the day before I received this letter, I took a personal day, just to stay home and relax and focus on my projects. That particular day, as I sat in meditation, I decided not to plan out the day, but to let the day unfold. I then felt an urge to call Mary Anna and invite her for lunch or a walk. She chose the walk.

Mary Anna learned from her mother, part Native American and part African American. Her mother taught her about the Earth. So, whenever I talk with Mary Anna, I feel there is a deep reservoir of wisdom from which she draws. This training passes from one generation to the next, but I fear the link breaks in these last few generations. I yearn to know more of her wisdom.

We didn't have to go far for her to find wonder. As we walked in the cemetery/arboretum near my house, she demonstrated her deep reverence and love for the Earth. A drab end-of-winter day transformed into a walk into the miracles of life.

How did this happen? Mary Anna perfects the art of paying attention. The algae in the pond, the woodpecker holes in the bark, the geese, the burled oak, the insect paths on wood, wildflower names -- all fell under her loving gaze and consequently into mine. We had a wonderful walk, and the next day, I received this letter from Gaia

The Letter

Dear Nancy,
    Thank you for taking me very seriously. When you slow down and pay attention, you will discover mysteries abound everywhere in my creation.

Weren't you so happy to spend some time with our friend, Mary Anna Robinson, yesterday? Didn't she teach you about me? In just a couple hours or so, you gathered her wisdom. I watched you.

What did she do that taught you? Let's see. Wasn't she just paying attention? She focused your attention on aspects of Me that you would have overlooked.

She pointed out the bright green algae in the pond and told you spring is coming now. She taught you to read the signs in nature.

She carefully observed the tree trunk riddled with holes and told you, "The woodpeckers like this tree." She taught you to look more closely.

She talked about the geese near your path and explained that they mate for life. Although the ones you saw were all males, she said. They have beautiful markings and the females are all brown. She taught you about love in nature.

She pointed out a patch of burled oak, little knobs of wood poking out of earth and explained to you that insects in the roots cause these to crop up and that makes beautiful wood. She taught you that beauty often comes in unexpected ways.

She picked up a piece of wood, a broken branch, and showed you the insect paths created on the bare limb. She talked about recreating this design on a wooden thimble. "I'm a woodcarver," she told you. And she taught you to be creative in art with nature.

She marveled at the wildflowers with you. The tiny white, purple, and yellow flowers covered the ground by the limestone cliffs. You wondered about their names. She said she would go home and look them up and figure that out. She taught you to keep learning, using the resources you have to comprehend more.

There in just a short space of the afternoon, you learned so much from Mary Anna about me.

So, Nancy, once again, I encourage you to slow down. Take time. Observe. Do you understand you live within miracle after miracle unfolding? I think you do now. I am so glad.

Love, Gaia

My Response

And so, although I thought I knew why the Earth recommended I learn from Mary Anna, I didn't really comprehend how much she could teach me, until we went for this walk on that day. Ever so gently, the Earth pointed this out to me in this letter, as she retraced the path we shared. And she pointed out what I learned from Mary Anna. She taught me to read the signs in nature, to look more closely and pay attention, to see love in nature, to realize that beauty comes in unexpected ways, to be creative with art in nature, and to continue to learn about nature.

Wow! My heart leaps, my love blossoms, my soul rejoices. I think of that worship song, "Holy ground, we're standing on holy ground." And I know that the Earth calls me to experience all of life in this way.

I sit here, listening, and her voice sounds pure and good. "Slow down, take time, observe." I want to tell her, "I'm trying, Gaia. I really am." But I make mistakes. My broken hand reminds me that I haven't quite achieved her hopes for me.

I think back over my year. From Seattle to Hocking Hills, from Lake Erie to Ireland, from Myrtle Beach to Dallas, after my morning meditation she writes again and again, awakening my joy. I feel so blessed with her messages that are changing me slowly from within. I seek out opportunities to dance. I cultivate the Earth. I do slow down and savor the moment.

Yesterday, on the way to work, I picked a daffodil out of my yard, and put it in a glass to observe all day long on my desk. I picked it up and enjoyed the fragrance several times. I took a picture of it with my cell phone and shared it with my Facebook friends, commenting, "Picked this from our yard this morning. Exquisite fragrance and absolutely perfect. Happy Spring!" As I check back this morning, 38 of my friends liked it, too.

Yes, Gaia, I am beginning to be much more aware that I live within miracle after miracle unfolding. And like you, I am so glad.

A Letter to the Reader from Nancy

Dear Reader,
 Thank you for taking time to listen to my Letters from the Earth. I hope that perhaps they will make a difference in your life, as they do in mine.
 As I reread them now, I realize that a lot of the Earth's message concerns taking time to really appreciate and enjoy life as it comes. So here are a few of the gems of instruction that you might want to incorporate into your everyday life.
 If you journal, I suggest reflecting on each of the gems separately. Answer these questions: To what extent is this "gem" already a part of my approach to life? What were sometimes I remember doing this? How did that enhance my life? What small step could I take today to make this practice more a part of my life?

1. **Be aware. Take time to really notice the people, experiences, seasons, and natural world.** When life becomes routine, we often don't really notice what the Earth calls the "miraculous" in every moment. You might try a practice of journaling to help reflect on the experiences of your day. Take a walk regularly outdoors to observe what's happening.

2. **Slow down.** If you are like me, you may be trying to squeeze the most out of every day, and going fast seems the best way to do this sometimes. But experiment with slowing down. Maybe this means intentionally putting fewer things on your "to do" list for the day so you'll have a sense of spaciousness as your work. Maybe this means taking a Sabbath every week. I have one friend who stays home one day of the weekend and makes no plans for that day. Maybe this means walking slowly to observe. Maybe this means taking a nap. I still remember that day I stopped at Old Man's Cave and lay down for a nap. Taking a nap restored and refreshed me so much.

3. **Appreciate people.** If you take time to affirm and appreciate the people in your life, you will feel happier and they will feel happier around you. Sometimes we tend to focus on the negative, but if you look for the positives, there is much to compliment. When it comes to caring for the Earth, applaud everyone you see making efforts to do something. The Earth says, "This is the best you can do." I find it's a very fun thing to do as well.

4. **Savor food.** Remember that Garden Party I had in my back yard? Surrounded by flowers, we had wonderful salads and I really took time to savor each bite. So often we rush our meals, watching TV, reading, catching up on emails, playing electronic games. Try mindfully eating. Enjoy each bite. Not only will you find you digest your food better, but you will be less likely to overeat. Conversation over meals can be great, but try eating in silence sometimes, too. Give thanks for those who made your meal possible. Imagine and visualize the process

from farm to table. When you really consider the origins of your food, you will be totally mesmerized with your bounty.

5. **Get outdoors and observe nature.** Whether you live in the middle of a city or out in the country, there are miracles to be discovered outside each day. A five-minute break for a short walk can lift your spirit. Consider an ant, a plant, a flower. A walk in the woods will enhance your oxygen level and refresh you immensely. Like Mary Anna, observe carefully what's going on and learn more about what you see. If you want to listen for messages, practice Lectio Divina with the earth. First, read (*lectio*) nature. Look for something that jumps out at you or shimmers. What catches your attention? Second, meditate (*meditatio*) on this aspect of nature. What do you see there? How does it speak to you? What message is there for you? Third, pray (*oratio*) about it and ask God to help you incorporate this message into your life and fourth, contemplate (*contemplativo*) for a while, just sitting in silence. It's amazing the messages that come when you take time to open the "Holy Book" of nature in this way.

6. **Wake up.** I would encourage you to awaken from your slumbers and become aware of what is happening to our environment. If you don't know much about what's going on, you owe it to yourself and future generations to begin to wake up to the reality of what we are doing to the Earth. I have put together a list of ten books that you can read that will lay it all out for you. While it's difficult to hear and to know, I do believe the Earth when she tells us it's not too late. Take advantage of all the information available to you. Take time to learn so that you might help change the course of history.

7. **Speak.** When I first began to sense the crisis of the environment, I didn't believe that I could make a difference. In a workshop I attended, we made prayer bracelets to encourage us to pray for the Earth each day.

We chose a multi-colored bead that would remind us to pray for the people, and particularly for ourselves and what action we might be able to take for the Earth. I remember my skepticism. But each day, I wore my bracelet, and I prayed, and I asked God to help me do what I could do. Slowly, I began to become aware of things. At the time, I was taking my class on leading contemplative small groups and retreats. I planned a week of classes focusing on the earth as a starting point for meditation and led the classes at a retreat center in the mountains of Washington State. I incorporated these practices into a small group I led back at home. When my husband began to participate in the Citizens' Climate Lobby, I joined his efforts. I began to write my second novel with an Earth theme, naming my main character after Thomas Berry, a priest who figured out in the 1980s that the biggest task of our time, which he dubbed "The Ecozoic Era", would be to change the way we are using the earth in a destructive manner. And when I started to receive letters from the Earth, I kept listening. And when my writing coach suggested the letters could become a book, I started working on it. Don't assume that you can do nothing. Open yourself to possibilities. Like me, I believe you will find there are many things you can do. Together, we will change the course of history.

8. **Live in the moment.** Like me, I imagine **you've** heard this before. And, like for me, I imagine it may be very hard for you to do this. **But consider that the only moment you will ever have is now.** Let each moment be sacred. Enjoy and savor the time that is yours. Slow down. Be aware. Appreciate. Savor. Observe. Wake up. Speak. All of these practices are about living in the moment. Time and time again in these letters, the Earth lifted my spirit by telling me to enjoy and fully experience life. We are called to enjoy the miracle of being alive in each moment.

9. **Dance. Get up and get moving!** As I read over these letters, this directive seems to come in almost every letter. I think the Earth calls us to inhabit our bodies and

have fun with them. Put on some of your favorite music and start moving. How does that make you feel? Work to overcome your inhibitions. Take a dance or exercise class where you can learn some new steps. Be bold. Laugh. Enjoy your one wild and precious life. If you can't move your whole body, use what you can. Let your hand dance, or your eyes, or your heart!

10. **Love.** And most of all, the Earth calls you to fall in love with yourself, with other people, with all of nature and with her, with your creator, Gaia God. I find in meditation, I begin to become aware of our unity and experience this love in a visceral way. However you might find ways to experience and share love, I encourage you to do that. Perhaps this comes through spiritual disciplines, reading scriptures, acts of service, and time in prayer. Perhaps through practice and making time for yourself, your friends and family, your God, you will grow in the ability to love. That's the bottom line, that's what it's all about.

Acknowledgements

I give thanks foremost to God for entrusting me with this message to share. Thanks to Joanna Macy and Chris Johnstone for the recommendation to write a letter to yourself from the Earth. Thanks to my writing coach, Kathie Giorgio (All Writers' Workshop and Workplace) who recommended I write this book and then helped me craft it into a memoir. Thanks to all my friends and family who have read and affirmed the voice of hope shining through these letters. Deep gratitude to my spiritual director, Loretta Farmer, who always affirms that the Earth is speaking to both me and many others today. Finally, thanks Rebecca Benston of Higher Ground Books and Media for publishing this book and enabling me to offer it to you.

Resources

Bibliography

Berry, Thomas. **Dream of the Earth.** 1988

Cannato, Judy. **Field of Compassion: How the New Cosmology is Transforming Spiritual Life:** Sorin Books, 2010

Cannato, Judy. **Radical Amazement: Contemplative Lessons from Black Holes, Supernovas, and other Wonders of the Universe.** Notre Dame, Indiana, Sorin Books, 2006.

Fischer, Kathleen. **Loving Creation. Christian Spirituality, Earth-Centered and Just.** New Jersey: Paulist Press, 2009. "Sacred Reading of the Book of Nature" pp.117-120.

Flinchbaugh, Nancy. **Revelation in the Cave.** Springfield, Ohio: Spiritual Seedlings, 2012. **Revelation at the Labyrinth**: eLectio Publishing, 201

Forest, Jim. **Praying with Holy Icons.** New York: Orbis Books, 2008

Hall, Thelma. **Too Deep for Words: Rediscovering Lectio Divina.** New York: Paulist Press, 1988

Hamma, Robert M. **Earth's Echo: Sacred Encounters with Nature.** Notre Dame, Indiana: Sorin, 2002.

Keating, Thomas. **Open Mind, Open Heart.** New York: Amity House, 1986.

Koch, Carl and Joyce Heil. **Created in God's Image: Meditating on our Body.** Winona, MN: St. Mary's Press 1991.

Kubler-Ross, Elisabeth. **On Death and Dying.** New York: Routledge, 1969

Macy, Joanna and Chris Johnstone. **Active Hope: How to Face the Mess We're in without Going Crazy.** Novato, California: New World Library, 2012.

May, Gerald. *The Awakened Heart.* San Francisco: HarperCollins, 2005.

The Wisdom of the Wilderness. San Francisco: HarperOne, 2009.

Experiencing the Healing Power of Nature. San Francisco: Harper, 2006.

O'Donohue, John. *Anam Cara: A Book of Celtic Wisdom.* San New York: HarperCollins, 2009

Pope Francis. *Encyclical Letter Laudato Si of the Holy Father Francis on Care for our Common Home.* The Vatican, 2015.

Rogin, Neal. *The Awakening Universe.* (Film)

Ryan, Thomas, editor. *Reclaiming the Body in Christian Spirituality.* NJ: Paulist Press, 2004.

Ryan, Thomas. *Prayer of Heart and Body: Meditation and Yoga as Christian Spiritual Practice.* Mahwah, NJ: Paulist Press 1995.

Salyers, Mary Jane. *Appalachian Daughter.* CreateSpace: 2012

Swimme, Brian. *The Hidden Heart of Cosmos: Humanity and the New Story.* New York: Orbis Books, 1996.

Vaughn-Lee, Lwelleyn. *Spiritual Ecology: The Cry of the Earth.* Point Reyes Station, California: The Golden Sufi Center, 2016.

Wilder, Thornton. "Our Town,"1938.

Wolpert, Daniel. *Creating a Life with God: The Call of Ancient Prayer Practices.* Nashville: Upper Room: 2003.

Organizations/Websites

AllWriters' Workplace and Workshop, LLC. http://www.allwritersworkshop.com/
Bergamo and the Marianist Environmental Center. http://www.bergamocenter.org/
Citizens' Climate Lobby works to build political will for a

sustainable world. A great organization which has been doubling annually. They lobby for a revenue neutral carbon fee and dividend which could reduce carbon emissions by 50% and spur the market to develop alternative fuels while growing the economy. www. citizensclimatelobby.org.

Climate Pledge Ohio Website. **www.climatepledgeohio.weebly.com**.

Springfield CultureFest at City Hall Plaza, last Saturday of September. www.springfieldohio.org/culturefest/

Gary Geis School of Dance. http://www.garygeisdance.org/

Lakeside Environmental Stewardship Society (LESS). http://www.lakesideohio.com/community/organizations/lakeside-environmental-stewardship-society

Marianist Environmental Education Center. http://meec.udayton.edu

NASA Website. http://science.nasa.gov/astrophysics/focus-areas/what-is-dark-energy

Pachamama Alliance. http://www.pachamama.org/

Shalem Institute for Spiritual Formation in Washington, DC offers programs on leading Christian contemplative small groups and retreats, spiritual direction training, training for clergy and other seminars and retreats. A great organization that helps develop the Christian contemplative experience in churches worldwide. **www.shalem.org**

Solas Bhride Centre and Hermitages. http://solasbhride.ie/

Spiritual Seedlings. www.spiritualseedlings.com

The Spirituality Network in Columbus, Ohio offers many retreats and workshops. **www.spiritualitynetwork.org**

Veriditas. http://veriditas.org/

The Places

Brookgreen Gardens. www.brookgreen.org/
Cliffs of Moher. www.cliffsofmoher.ie/
Ferncliff Cemetery and Arboretum.

ferncliffcemetery.org/
   Hocking Hills State Park/ Old Man's Cave.
hockinghills.com/old_mans_cave.html
   Huntington Beach State Park.
www.huntingtonbeachstatepark.net/
   Lakeside, Ohio. www.lakesideohio.com/
   Newgrange. www.newgrange.com/

Other titles from Higher Ground Books & Media:

Wise Up to Rise Up by Rebecca Benston

A Path to Shalom by Steen Burke

From a Hole in My Life to a Life Made Whole by Janet Kay Teresa

Overcomer by Forrest Henslee

Miracles: I Love Them by Forest Godin

32 Days with Christ's Passion by Mark Etter

The Magic Egg by Linda Phillipson

The Tin Can Gang by Chuck David

Whobert the Owl by Mya C. Benston

For His Eyes Only by John Salmon

Out of Darkness by Stephen Bowman

Knowing Affliction and Doing Recovery by John Baldasare

Add these titles to your collection today!

http://highergroundbooksandmedia.com